'Round Lake Erie: A Bicyclist's Tour Guide,
2nd Edition

Harvey Botzman

'Round Lake Erie

A Bicyclist's Tour Guide

2nd Edition

Harvey Botzman

Cyclotour Guide Books
Rochester, New York
2004

'Round Lake Erie: A Bicyclist's Tour Guide, 2nd Edition
© Harvey Botzman, 1994, 2003, 2004.

Cyclotour Guide Books
PO Box 10585, Rochester, New York 14610-0585 USA
http://www.cyclotour.com
cyclotour@cyclotour.com
Tel. & Fax: 585 244-6157

Other books by the author:
'Round Lake Ontario: A Bicyclist's Tour Guide
'Round Lake Michigan: A Bicyclist's Tour Guide
'Round Lake Huron: A Bicyclist's Tour Guide
'Round Lake Superior: A Bicyclist's Tour Guide
Erie Canal Bicyclist & Hiker Tour Guide
Finger Lakes Bicyclist's Tour Guide
Long Distance Bicycle Touring Primer

Disclaimers:
The author, publisher, wholesale and retail purveyor, and library owner of this book and its contents; and government units/ agencies on whose roads you bicycle are not responsible for your bicycling habit, bicycle and any accidents which might occur.
They encourage users of this *Guide* to wear a helmet; use a mechanically correct bicycle; use reflectors; use lights even during daylight hours; wear clothing which is readily visible to motorists, pedestrians and others; watch for other vehicles; position yourself and your bicycle correctly on a roadway or trail; and obey all traffic laws, rules and regulations.
Road and trail conditions change. The routes suggested herein may be altered due to road and trail work; surface conditions; or your need to explore. Every effort has been made to provide accurate information.

Library of Congress Control Number (LCCN): 2003091855

ISBN: 1-889602-23-X

10 9 8 7 6 5 4 3 2 1

To Friends

From the past,
current and in the future
with whom I travel
through life
experiencing
the joy of new adventures.

'Round Lake Erie: A Bicyclist's Tour Guide, 2nd Ed.

Harvey Botzman

CONTENTS

ACKNOWLEDGEMENTS

This series of books would not have been written without my
    father and mother, Samuel and Lillian Botzman, teaching
    me how to explore and enjoy the world.

Thanks to the encouragement of my sister and brother in law
    Gail and Gerry; nieces and their husbands Randi and
    Ron, Bonnie and Mark; and great-nephews Alex, Jordan
    and Zachary I have been able to revise the Great Lakes
    Bicycle Tour Guide Series.

The business advice and traveling experiences of Joe and
    Sylvia Baron was invaluable. Uncle Abraham and aunt
    Celia Aaroni's enthusiasm for this endeavor lead me to
    continue writing.

It was my friends and their children to whom I owe immense
    gratitude for their support, criticism and ability to take me
    away from staring at a computer monitor! Thanks, Ed,
    Martha, Eli and Emmy Awad; Jim, Becky, Jenny and
    Jimmy Parks; Jeff Schwartz and Judy; Pat Townsend,
    Gervais and Lori Pivarnik; Bob and his sons Nathaniel
    and Tommy Howe.

The school administrators who have kept me employed as a
    per diem substitute teacher and thus able to eat. Bar-
    bara, Luwon, Kim, Paul, Deesure, Bill, Marilyn and others
    Hire me as a full time teacher, the students will gain from
    my knowledge base and experience. I'll have more effi-
    cient time management to allow me to write more.

Boyhood friends who bicycled with me Larry, Barry, David,
    Ron, Richard, Billy and cousin Donny might be the
    originators of this series of tour guides.

Thanks.

Harvey Botzman

June 30, 2003
May 15, 2004
Rochester, New York

PREFACE

Most North Americans take the proximity of having one fifth of the earth's supply of fresh water for granted. Lake Erie, as with the four other Great Lakes are relatively unknown to many North Americans.

The Great Lakes region are neither viewed as exotic vacation destinations nor as the playgrounds of the rich and famous. This is the opposite of how they were seen in the late 19th and early 20th centuries. Presidents, industrialists, Wall Street tycoons, entertainers, progressive middle class intellectuals and farmers all used the Lakes as their primary vacation playground.

Little known but denigrated, Lake Erie has played a major part in the history and development of North America. On its waters Great Britain and the United States waged war.

The climate created by this large mass of water contributed to the mid-west's development as a prime agricultural area.

On its shores factories developed to produce myriad products for the North American and the world economy. The result of this industrial development was an extremely polluted Lake. With the imposition of water quality standards and less polluting industrial processes lake Erie's water has become clearer and cleaner.

Enjoy Lake Erie as you cyclotour. Swim, scuba dive, water ski and loll on its beaches. Enjoy its historical and cultural attractions. Bicycle tourists are well respected in this area.

TOUR PREPARATION

Contents

Traveler Note

This chapter, *Tour Preparation*, has grown from 12 pages to 25 pages. You really do not need to carry these pages on your cyclotour. Save some weight and space. Rip out these pages; cyclotour; and paste them back in when you return home.

Types of Bicycle Touring

I travel as a self-contained bicycle tourist. I cyclotour in this manner to view the world at its level as well as for economic reasons. The philosophical concept of self-reliance has a direct bearing on my mode of travel.

Other people cyclotour with only a credit card, an emergency repair kit, some snacks, and a few pieces of clothing.

Still others travel with a sag wagon containing all their equipment, friends or family members.

Some people travel alone some with family or friends. Many folks prefer to cyclotour with commercial or non-profit organized tours.

It really doesn't matter how you define your form of cyclotouring. You made a choice to travel by bicycle rather than by car or public transportation. You will meet people who state, ...*since I first rode a bicycle I've always wanted to bicycle tour.* You're cyclotouring and they're still waiting to bicycle tour!

In American and Canadian society we tend to define and classify what we do. In my mind bicycle touring is cyclotouring is bicycle touring. For others the following definitions of cyclotouring can help to sort out the type of bicycle touring which best meets their needs and wants.

Self-contained (self-reliant) Cyclotouring is when the bicyclist, (alone or with others) carries sufficient equipment to maintain the bicyclist(s) for the entire tour period. The equipment includes but is not limited to camping gear, clothing, personal gear, tools, and food. Obviously, consumables (food, *etc.*) will be replenished as the tour progresses.

Partially Loaded Cyclotouring is when the bicyclist carries emergency sleeping/camping equipment, basic repair equipment, a limited amount of clothing and personal items, snacks, or one meal's worth of food. A combination of commercial lodging and preparing one's own food or camping and eating in restaurants is considered partially loaded cyclotouring.

Credit Card Cyclotouring is for bicyclists who want to be least encumbered with *stuff*! A credit card or debit card is necessary! Travelers checks will suffice! Only small panniers are needed along with a lock; a wallet with credit cards; and a small amount of cash! Meals are eaten in restaurants. Lodging is at motels, b&bs or hostels. The cyclotourist travels by charging everything to the credit card or paying cash. Hopefully the tourist doesn't forget to pay the bills!

Segment Cyclotouring is completing a long distance tour over a period of time with breaks to return home. The bicyclist starts each segment at the point where the previous segment was completed.

Personal Sag Wagon Cyclotouring is a touring mode in which the food, camping and bicycle specific equipment is carried in a sag wagon. A spouse or friend functions as the sag wagon driver. The bicyclist(s) carries the minimum* amount of snacks, water, repair equipment, and some rain gear. Many times lodging for sag wagon bicycle tourists is at motels or b&bs rather than campsites. Bicyclist(s) and sag wagon meet at predetermined places for food, fun, and lodging.

Day Tripping is when an individual or a group travel for one day on a short round trip tour of a specific area. Usually these travelers carry the bare minimum amount of equipment and eat in restaurants.

Arranged Cyclotouring is when all long distance touring arrangements (with or without sag wagon support) are made by a non-profit or commercial bicycle tour company. Cyclotourists who participate in arranged touring have memorable experiences less the hassles associated with making all the arrangements themselves. They usually enjoy meeting and interacting with people who have similar interests.

Bikepacking is off road cyclotouring. Usually the object is to establish a camping spot and mt. bike on trails from that base camp.

Guerrilla Camping is finding a beautiful secluded place, off the road and using it as your camp site. The guerrilla camper makes every effort to obtain permission to camp if there is an indication that the site is on private property.

Friends, Family and the Passionate Cyclotourist

How to convince your non-cycling family members or friends to help you exercise your cyclotouring fantasy without breaking up the relationship!

1.   Make certain all family/friends have bicycles.

2.   Plan your tour so that the first few overnight stops are 20-30 miles apart. This will allow you to spend time with your loved ones or friends while you tour.

3.   The *passionate cyclotourist* bicycles to each overnight stop. At the overnight stopping point, the dedicated cyclist joins the other members of the touring group for an hour or two of recreational bicycling. Enjoy your vacation!

4.   The passionate cyclist suggests to the other vacationers that one semi-dedicated bicyclist accompanies him/her on a portion of the next day's ride between overnight stops.

5.   The sag wagon meets you and the co-rider at an intermediate point; picks up the co-rider who normally would not want to bicycle the entire distance between stops. You, the experienced cyclotourist, continues riding the entire distance to the next overnight stop.

6.   Continue doing this for a few days and your family and friends will start enjoying *total* bicycle touring with you.

7.   Alternatively, purchase a tandem!

Breakdown Cruise

At least two weeks before your tour begins take a short trial tour. Pack everything you *intend* to take on your long distance cyclotour. Include, in your panniers, what you *think* might be needed on your cyclotour. Ride twenty or thirty miles to a nearby campground. Stay overnight. Make notes on how you and your bike traveled.

When you return home, toss out everything which was superfluous to your weekend trip. Be vicious! Be heartless! "***Less is more***," Mies Van der Rohr said. Truer words were never stated in regard to cyclotouring. The less you load into your panniers the lighter your bike and the more enjoyable your tour!

Equipment

There are many bicyclists with more miles under their toes than me. They might carry more equipment than I do. My needs are very basic while cyclotouring. Your needs are different.

One bicycle, kind of essential and I use an old one:
    18 speed, triple crank (24/40/52 x 13/34).

Right Rear Pannier	Left Rear Pannier
Tent	Stove inside a 1 qt. pan
Tent Poles	Fuel Bottle
Mattress Pad	First Aid Kit
Tools & Lights	Maps, misc. papers
Personal Items	Personal Items
1/2 "U" lock	1/2 "U" lock

Sleeping bag on top of the rear rack.

Right Front Pannier	Left Front Pannier
Clothing	Food

Total weight = ~37 lb./17 kg. including panniers.

For aerodynamic and theft reasons, I try to have very few items *blowin' in the wind!*
The load is balanced, left and right sides, front and rear. I shift items between panniers to better balance the load.
I use both sets of panniers because I'm small and light weight! If all the weight is on the rear wheels I lose some steering control.
This pannier set up changes if I do not use front panniers. Then the rear panniers are balanced by a handlebar bag containing a limited number of heavy items: "U" lock, camera, snacks (fruit weights a lot), rain wear, towel, and bathing suit.

Roads
State Highways in New York, Pennsylvania, Ohio, and Michigan are usually surfaced with asphalt. State maintained roads have a striped paved shoulder of at least 4 ft. (1.2 m.) In this *Tour Guide* these roads are termed respectively, NY, PA, OH, and M + [Road number] in the text.
Provincial Highways (King's Highways) in Ontario are major roads with an asphalt or cement surface. They may or may not have a paved shoulder. These roads are termed PH + [Road number].
State, Provincial, county and municipal roads used in this book usually have a chip sealed surface. These roads may have a shoulder and then again they may not. If there is a shoulder it will be narrow and either gravel or mowed grass. These roads are termed CR + [Road number] or have a name.
The trails used in this *Tour Guide* are usually surfaced with stone dust. Technically stone dust is stone <.125 in. (<.32 cm.) in diameter. Generally the stone used is shale or ground metamorphic rock. The stone dust comes from two sources, quarries and street sweepings. The street sweepings have the added advantage of containing minute non-polluting amounts of salt left over from winter road salting. This small amount of salt inhibits the growth of vegetation on the trail.

Bicycles
Your Bike vs. a Touring Bike
For most cyclotourists their tried and true bike will suffice for this tour. We do suggest that you use new slightly wider tires for this tour. There are several sections of the route where you might have to ride on a gravel or grass shoulder. A wider tire with a slightly more defined tread pattern will provide more steering control in such instances.
It is *fit* not the type of bicycle which is important for successful

cyclotouring (or any type of bicycling). An improper fit of your body to a bicycle will make your bicycle tour a horror. A proper fit of your body to a bicycle will make your tour a joy.
You can use any type of bike, with some modifications, for this or any other cyclotour. You can place racks, panniers, lights, fenders, different tires, and different gearing on a hybrid, sport tourer, mt. bike or even a racing bike and still successfully tour! Yes, purists! People do successfully tour on department and discount store bicycles.
Traditional touring bicycles with long chain stays and a full range of gears are a rare sight in bike shops. Only a few major bike manufacturers make touring bikes. An additional fifteen or so custom builders make touring bikes. If you think you really need one, have your local bike shop order it.
The primary differences between a touring bicycle and a recreational bike or mt. bike are in the chain stay length; head tube angle; frame flex; sufficient frame strength to carry a load; stronger or more spokes; and having sufficient busses for attaching racks, water bottles, *etc*.
A touring bike usually has chainstays which are ~18 in./45.7 cm. or more in length. The head tube angle on a touring bike tends to be ~73°. Yes, all these technical specifications do make for a more comfortable long distance ride.
Bicycle manufacturers put all sorts of *do dads* on recreational bikes to make them appear as touring bicycles. Do a bit of research if you are planning to purchase a touring bicycle.

Mt. Bikes

A mt. bike makes a fine touring machine! Yes, traditional touring bike riders, they do! True, a few modifications are necessary to make a Mt. bike a more efficient touring bike. None the less, they make comfortable touring bikes.
A mt. bike with a front suspension fork generally can not use front panniers. This means that all the weight of your *stuff* will be on the rear wheel. Use a handle bar bag and place some of the weightier items (U lock) in it to help balance the load.
Or change the front fork! If you do this, make certain that the new suspension fork has busses for attaching front racks. Several manufacturers now make front forks specifically designed for attaching front racks. Front panniers really are not necessary if you limit the amount of *stuff* you take on your cyclotour! *Less is More!*
A number of rack manufacturers make special Mt. bike front and rear racks which can be used with front and rear suspended frames. Ask about these racks at your local bike shop or send Cyclotour Guide Books a letter or email. We try to

maintain information files to answer your touring questions.
Mt. bikes with short chain stays may present a problem with rear
panniers. Your heels may continually strike the rear panniers
as you pedal. If this occurs on your bike, move the panniers
a few inches or centimeters rearward. Carefully pack your
rear panniers with the heaviest items centered over the axle.
Mt. bike handle bars and handle bar mounted shifters are
designed for constant shifting on difficult terrain. In general
cyclotourists do not shift often but need to change their hand
positions often to relieve numbness.
Don't go out and purchase a new set of shifters or handlebars! A
simple and inexpensive mt. bike modification is to add bar
ends.. These bar ends will allow you to use your current
shifters and provide additional hand positions to relieve
numbness. A new type of bolt on Mt. bike bar end even has
the traditional dropped curved section. A number of
cyclotourists use bolt on aero bars to provide even more hand
positions.

Tires
Use a set of the multipurpose touring tires. Multipurpose touring
tires are efficient for negotiating smooth asphalt, stone dust
and will allow you to successfully explore any dirt roads which
strike your fancy.
Slick no tread tires are not suitable for touring. Occasionally you
might have to go off the roadway and onto a gravel or grass
shoulder. Slicks on such surfaces will provide a greater
chance for you to wipe out!
A set of fairly wide, >28 mm. (~1 in.), touring or hybrid tires with a
well defined (but not knobby) tread pattern will be well worth
their premium price by having sufficient tread to slough off
roadway irregularities. The well defined side tread pattern will
provide excellent traction and the smoother central road tread
pattern will provide low rolling resistance.
Although mt. bikes make fine touring machines for this tour,
knobby treaded mt. bike tires are not useful for traveling on
asphalt or chip seal. Knobby tires have too much rolling
resistance and wear out very fast touring on road surfaces.

Gearing!
A triple chain ring with a relatively small inner chain ring is useful
for traversing hills.
Mt. Bike gearing usually provides a full range of choices for street
and off road use. Mountain bikers might find that the higher
gears used for road travel are not on their bike. One
relatively easy way to obtain a more suitable gear
configuration is to change the chain rings. Simply bolt on a

large chain ring with more teeth (Don't forget to remove the current chain ring!). You might have wider steps between some gear stops but nothing which presents undue problems. Keep the small chain ring, you'll need it for the hills!

Given the chain rings on newer bikes (road and mountain), this might not be a simple modification. Check with an experienced bicycle mechanic at a good bike shop before replacing the chain rings or freewheel.

Other Bits & Pieces

A first aid kit is a necessity.

Rain gear for the inevitable rain shower is a must.

Warm clothing for chilly mornings/evenings and after a rain shower will help prevent hypothermia.

Clothing is bulky and surprisingly weighs a lot. Do not take too much clothing, Layer your clothing. Laundromats are available in small and large towns.

H_2O must be carried. Dehydration is the prime malady of bicyclists. Drink at least 8-12 fl. oz. (235-355 ml.) of water per half or three quarters of an hour. It is far better to drink more water than less water. You can add those high energy/electrolyte replacement substances/drinks to your water bottle but good old H_2O and some fruit will be just as effective for the majority of cyclotourists.

Equipment Lists

Do not take too much! *Less is more!* Excess weight due to excess equipment, clothing, tools, and food make a bicycle tour a drudgery rather than a pleasure. There are sufficient supply depots along the way. A Post Office is always available to send *stuff* home!

The *Equipment Lists* can help you plan and choose the items you need on your tour. The *Lists* are simply provided. You make the decision what to pack in your panniers. Base your equipment decisions on the type of cyclotouring you are doing—fully loaded to credit card—and your need for *stuff*. You will be able to purchase *stuff* along your route. You will be able to send home anything which is superfluous.

The Equipment Lists are particularly useful when crossing international borders. The Customs agent may want to see a list of what is in your panniers. Simply show the agent the Equipment Lists and have the agent stamp the Lists. You'll save time upon reentry.

Balance your load, front and rear; right and left sides.

Do not overload your bicycle.

Climate Factors in Selected Cities on Lake Erie					
City	Month				
	May	June	July	Aug.	Sept.
Buffalo Ft. Erie	48-66/3.4 9-19/8.5	57-75/3.8 14-24/9.7	62-80/3.1 17-27/7.9	60-78/3.9 16-26/9.8	53-70/3.8 12-21/9.7
Erie PA	49-67/3.3 9-19/8.5	59-76/4.3 15-24/10.9	64-80/3.3 18-27/8.3	63-79/4.2 17-26/10.7	56-72/4.7 13-22/12.0
Cleveland	48-69/3.5 9-21/8.9	58-77/3.9 14-25/9.9	62-81/3.5 17-27/8.9	61-79/3.7 16-26/9.4	54-72/3.8 12-22/9.6
Toledo	53-74/3.0 12-23/7.6	63-83/3.8 17-28/9.8	68-87/3.1 20-31/7.9	66-84/3.0 19-29/7.5	59-77/2.6 15-25/6.6
Windsor	48-68/3.0 9-20/7.6	53-77/3.7 12-25/9.7	63-82/3.5 17-28/8.5	61-81/3.8 16-27/8.6	53-73/3.4 12-23/8.7

Key: Temperature range in degrees F/average precipitation in inch.
Temperature range in degrees C/average precipitation in cm.

Climate

During the summer (June-September) the climate of Lake Erie is
perfect for bicycling. It is in the marginal months, March-May
and October-November when the climate presents the most
notable problems.

Wind! The bane of cyclists! Generally the wind blows from the
Northwest or West.

A climate factor called, *lake effect* influences the land mass
surrounding large lakes creating micro-climate areas
bordering a lake. Lake effect areas have a different climate
than a location one or two miles away from a large body of
water. You might notice these micro climates as the route
verges away from the Lake. Lake effect also contributes to
the betterment of humankind by creating ideal conditions for
growing wine grapes and certain fruits like apricots in the
northern latitudes.

Precipitation and Temperature

Snow and cold weather may buffet the northern end of the Lake
during the marginal Spring and Autumn seasons.   Plan
accordingly.

In April and May the day time temperature range is from 45-70°F
(7-21°C) with rain a few days week. Rarely does it rain all
day.

Days during June, July and August most likely will be sunny and
clear with temperatures in the 73-85°F (23-30°C) range. It

rains during the summer about once a week but rarely for more than an hour or two. Evenings in late August can drop the temperature to the high 50s° F (10s° C.)   Early September days usually are warm with clear cloudless skies.

In late September the day time temperatures begin to descend to the 50-70°F (10-21°C) range.   Mid-October brings precipitation similar to September with slightly chillier day time temperatures. The added bonus of fantastic Fall foliage in mid to late September makes Lake Erie a prime cycling destinations for locals and visitors from afar.

Snow will most likely be falling and covering the ground in early March and late October. The snow during these months is heavy and wet. It may disappear after a day or two as the temperature rises and then again it might not.

Don't think snow hinders bicyclists from using the routes bordering the Lake. Road cyclists switch to mt. bikes with knobby tires or simply use tires with a more pronounced tread. They'll put on a few more layers of clothing to ride all year long. Mt. bikers claim that snow is like mud except colder.

Fuel for Body and Mind

I carry very little food. Some pasta, dehydrated sauce mixes, cereal, snacks, fresh fruit, and two bottles of water. Some type of food can be obtained readily along almost the entire route. There are several sections of the described route when you will not pass at least one small local grocery or convenience store. These areas are noted in the text.

Perishable products such as meat, cheese, milk or ice cream (the exception is yoghut) do not travel well in panniers. It is best to buy perishable products on a daily basis within a half hour of stopping to cook and eat them. Salmonella and other gastro-intestinal diseases can turn a delightful tour into a miserable experience. With a little common sense and care you should have few problems.

Without preaching, eating is important. Bicycling is a strenuous activity when you are touring everyday for a few weeks. Food and the correct foods to refuel and rebuild your depleted carbohydrate and protein supplies is of utmost importance.

I tend to eat more vegetables and carbohydrates (primarily pasta and rice) and less meat on my tours. These foods are relatively simple to store and prepare on the backpacking stove I use. I do eat my requisite beef, fish and chicken protein sources and they seem to taste even better mixed with farm fresh veggies.

Fresh vegetables and fruit can be bought at roadside stands. You will be missing a vital and satisfying culinary experience by not purchasing and eating fresh fruit and vegetables from the many farms and homeowners along the way.

Bananas and most citrus fruit, which tend to be staples of bicyclists, will have to be bought in groceries.

Take your fishing pole! Yup! There are fish in Lake Erie. Happy fish. You will encounter fisherpersons and they eat the fish they catch! Excellent trout, whitefish, bass, and other fish are found streams flowing into the Lake and the Lake itself.

If you are a fisherperson make certain you contact Ontario and Michigan for the proper regulations and licenses.

Take a chance eating at what appears to be a non-imposing restaurant or tavern. In most cases, you will be pleasantly surprised with a fine, hearty meal and a friendly atmosphere. Similarly, the village bakeries (real bakeries, not the supermarket variety) have superb delights!

A notation is made in the text of grocery stores, convenience stores, gas stations, and the more permanent farm stands along the route. In urban and suburban areas only the last supply depots before entering a relatively long stretch of road where there are few stores are they noted.

Many campgrounds have small stores which cater to campers. Usually, their selection is limited. Bear in mind that the concessionaires stock what is needed most by the campers in a given park. If the park has a large number of RV campers then there will be fewer groceries. Most RV campers come, to the park, prepared and have little need for purchasing groceries. Make life easy for yourself, plan ahead, stop at a grocery which is within a half hour of your next meal. Use the *Food List* to help plan your needs.

Keep everything light. Try not to buy canned goods. Use dehydrated sauces and fresh foods which will be consumed in a day or two. Price will rarely be a factor for the small quantities you will need.

A short paragraph about dehydrated food. You are not going to be traveling in an area which is totally isolated from civilization. Only a few 50 mi. (80 km.) stretches of the route are relatively devoid of humanity. Trees, grains, fruits, deer, and cows being the dominant inhabitants. Expensive backpacker type dehydrated food packets are not necessary. Search your grocery store for items like packets of sauces, veggie burgers in dehydrated form and pasta. Dehydrated foods—both those specifically designed for backpackers and those off the shelf in a grocery store—should be bought prior to the trip and tested for taste and preparation ease. There is nothing worse than looking forward to an easily prepared meal, making it and then discarding it for its foul taste.

One interesting *new* food available in your local grocery store is tuna fish in packets rather than cans.   The packet tuna weighs half as much as the canned tuna but contains the even more tuna: The water has been removed!

Similarly, dried filled tortellini are now readily available on grocery store shelves.   Instead of plain pasta these filled pasta delights will provide a hearty meal.   I even eat them in their dried form.

You might find that pasta with locally made cheese is just as easy to prepare as a box of macaroni and cheese.   It probably tastes better, too!

Carrying food

Plastic freezer bags are the simplest and easiest way to carry foods.   Purchase freezer rather than normal plastic bags, they hold up better.   You'll probably need a few different size bags.

Recently I've switched to carrying most of my food in plastic containers rather than plastic bags.   I thought there would be a significant weight and space difference but that does not appear to be true.   Plastic containers have the advantage of being easy to seal securely, not open and being more moisture proof.

Recipes

Basic foods which are always in my panniers:

    Pasta (spinach or avocado noodles, macaroni, etc.)
    Rice
    Cereal
    Jam, transferred to a plastic container, glass is heavy
    Coffee, fresh ground, in a plastic container
    Spice mixtures
    Yogurt. Yogurt keeps for several days.

Breakfast
Cereal w/yogurt
Fresh fruit
Coffee (ground or regular)
Backpacker coffee makers are now available.
Eggs, milk and other perishable items should be bought and used within an hour of purchase. Pancake mix is fine but fat (oil) is usually needed. Fats become rancid very quickly in warm weather. Besides clean up is much more difficult with these foods and you want to start riding as soon as possible.

Lunch
Sandwiches: Rolls or pita bread are easier to use and store than a loaf of bread. Peanut butter, jelly, cheese, fruit all on one sandwich. Packaged or fresh cut luncheon meat from a grocery is fine but remember that luncheon meat (as well as peanut butter) spoils very quickly. Use hard or semi-soft natural cheeses (cheddar, Swiss, parmesan) rather than soft or processed cheeses. The hard varieties will keep for several days.

Dinner
Pasta or rice.
Salad. Remember that lettuce and other vegetables are heavy and spoil baking in your panniers.
Soup:An easily prepared soup or stew can be made by dumping farm fresh vegetables along with a piece of chicken, ground beef or tofu into one pot.
Without the chicken (chicken stock spoils quickly) you can keep the soup overnight and use it for lunch the next day. If you make a vegetable soup and plan to use it for lunch the next day, boil it down to thicken the soup for over night storage and transport in you panniers. Of course you will need a container which seals securely. You can always thin the thickened soup with water.
Meats: If you're at a grocery within a half hour of making dinner, have the butcher put the meat into a plastic freezer bag then place that bag into a second bag packed with ice (usually the butcher supplies free ice). Do not use any ice which has come in contact with uncooked meat.
Many times during the Summer open flame fires are forbidden due to the danger of starting a forest fire.
Sauce
Sauces make meals interesting. Instead of carrying bottles or cans of pasta sauce use packets of different varieties of dehydrated sauce mixes (marinara, pesto, alfredo, Thai noodle, sweet and sour, etc.). These are found in almost any grocery store. They are lighter and easier to use than bottled

sauce. A packet of sauce can be used for two or three meals! Simply roll over the packet top and place it in a small plastic bag to store for another dinner or lunch. The dehydrated sauce mix can be sprinkled on top of sandwich *fixins* to provide additional taste treats.

One Pot Cooking: Drain the pasta but leave a bit of water in the pan. Add some of the sauce mix, stir and eat! Yogurt and peanut butter can be added to the pasta to make a sauce! Real simple preparation for hearty meal. Little clean up.

Most commercial sauce mixes contain too much salt for my taste. Bulk spices can be found in many grocery stores and natural food stores. You'll only need about .02 oz. (.5g.) of these bulk spices for 10 days of touring! Empty 35 mm film canisters make perfect bulk spice/sauce containers.

Gourmet eating at its finest!

Watch your calories; your carbohydrate, fat, and protein balance!

Drink sufficient water!

Eat enough carbohydrates to refuel your bod. Do not BONK!

Tools

I'm a fanatic about tools. I probably bring too many. After being stuck in some desolate places without a nut or screw of the right size or thread I try to be prepared for almost anything.

There are several sections of this route where you will be more than 75 mi. (120 km.) from a bike shop. The Post Office, UPS or a friendly motorist can easily transport a vital item to your campsite or lodging.

Although bicycle shops are located in major cities and towns, hardware stores and mass merchandisers abound. Most of these *substitute* bike shops will have something you can use for an emergency repair.

See the *Tool List* and make your own selection. Tools weigh a lot! Use discretion. The newer multiple use tools are great, provided they meet your needs. Test the way your tools work before loading them into your panniers. Combine tools; unscrew or cut off parts of tools you don't think you'll need.

Three patch kits, two spare tubes, a pump, hex wrenches, and screw drivers are the bare minimum tools you'll need. A spare tire is unnecessary on this trip. If your tire degenerates to the point of no return, simply call the nearest bike shop and have them post you a new one. The post office will deliver the package to your campsite, b&b, or motel! In the United States the Post Office delivers *Express Mail* on Sundays and holidays.

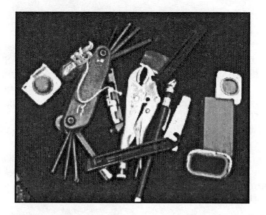

Personal Health & Safety

First Aid supplies are absolutely essential on a long distance tour. You can purchase ready made kits or you can assemble your own first aid supplies: gauze pads; bandages; adhesive tape; triangular bandage; general bacterial agent; sun screen; headache and muscle ache pills are the basic items. You will probably use all of these items. It may take two or three years before you use them but you will use them!

Be familiar with the danger signs associated with heat and muscle exhaustion; dehydration; hypothermia; and just being tired. Rest. Take care of yourself. Stop riding. If necessary go to a physician or hospital for treatment.

Helmet! Helmet! Always wear one! Even on rural roads and urban bikeways. If you have something to protect, your brains, wear a helmet. Pros wear bike helmets, amateurs don't.

Bicycles must be equipped with a rear red reflector (a flashing red rear light is OK if it also is a passive red rear reflector); a front reflector and a front light; aural warning device; and other basic safety equipment.

During the day, the rear red flashing light should be *on*. It helps to make you more visible to motorists. It marks you as an experienced safety conscious bicyclist.

Wear bright clothing.

When riding into the sun, wear clothing which will make you very visible to vehicle drivers. A t-shirt with dark stripes or a patterned shirt is perfect.

When riding with the sun at your back wear a top which will make you stand out from the scenery and sky. Use lots of reflective clothing during dusk, dawn and at night.

These safety items could save your life.

Lodging
All known bed & breakfasts and campgrounds are listed in the text
with their complete address and telephone numbers. There
may be some recently established lodgings which are not
listed. Conversely, there may be some listed lodgings which
are no longer in operation. These changes are the bane of
tour guide writers and are unavoidable. I have tried to keep
the listings up to date.
Consult the local tourist information office for a current lodging list.
Lodging facilities are not rated.
Use care to plan your overnight sojourns. Some villages and
hamlets along the way do not have formal places to sleep.
Guerrilla campers have a distinct advantage in this regard.

Maps
The maps in this book provide more than sufficient information for
you to cyclotour the route circumnavigating Lake Erie.
You can purchase large scale maps at most grocery or
bookstores along the route or have your hometown bookstore
order them. I recommend you cut up the large sheet regional
maps. You only need the panels which show the area
nearest the Lake.

People
Meeting people and speaking to them is part of the joy and
accessibility of cyclotouring. Unlike the Pacific Coast Bicycle
Route, a touring bicyclist is generally a rare sight around the
Great Lakes. People will ask about your trip. People will
offer help. Answer their queries with delight! Provide stories.
Weave tales which will make them jealous.

Public Transit
The rules for transporting a bicycle on buses, trains and planes
are changing every day. Consult with your public transportation carrier before you leave. Make certain that the carrier
notes that you will be transporting a bicycle in the reservations computer. If possible obtain written confirmation of the
rules under which the public transportation facility will carriage your bicycle.
A very efficient and enjoyable way to begin and end your cyclotour
is to travel to your start point or from your end point home via
train, airline or an inter-city bus. Of course if you live near the
Lake, just hop on your bike. This *Guide* is designed so that a
cyclotourist can begin and end at any point along the route.
Directions to and from the major train stations, airports and
bus terminals are provided in the text.

General Public Transit Rules

Each carrier—airline, bus and train companies—has specific rules regarding the transport of bicycles. All carriers specify that bicycles must be boxed and shipped as baggage. Trains and the airlines will sell you a box at the terminal. US bus companies do not stock bike boxes or bags at their terminals. Ontario Northern and Greyhound bus terminals in Canada do stock bike bags. Be prepared! Telephone ahead to confirm that the carrier has bike boxes/bags at its terminal.

If you are traveling to Lake Erie via public transportation then purchase the carrier's box or bag. These boxes are designed so that you only have to turn the handlebars and remove the pedals to fit a bicycle into the box. Very simple! You **must** have your own tools. Bicycle tools are not available at any terminals.

Using the carrier's bike box assures that the carrier can not claim your box was too weak for holding a bicycle. There is a moderate charge (~US$10-15.00) for the box.

Airlines

In general commuter airlines do <u>not</u> have facilities for the transport of bicycle boxes.

You will also have to pay an *extra* baggage charge on domestic United States and Canadian airline flights. This charge can be as high as US$ 80.00. A way of avoiding this ridiculous charge is to fly to Canada from the United States or vice versa. Airlines generally do not charge extra for bicycles on international flights.

Railroad

Amtrak and VIARail do not charge extra for transporting your bicycle, just for the bike box itself.

Port Huron and Sarnia are stops on the *International* train between Chicago and Toronto; a direct train goes from Chicago to Detroit; Windsor is the terminus for trains from Toronto traversing Ontario's Southwestern Peninsula along the north shore of Lake Erie. However these trains may not always have baggage cars or facilities to transport bikes.

One Amtrak train, the Lake Shore Limited, traverses the south shore of Lake Erie. This train does have baggage service.

Amtrak and VIARail only carry bicycles in baggage cars. This is significant! Not all Amtrak and VIARail trains and stations have baggage facilities! Make certain that both your originating and terminating train and station have baggage facilities. Otherwise your bike will be at one station and you at another.

Of course you could just carry your bike on to the coach if you have a folding bicycle or a Japanese *rinko bukuro* (bicycle bag, 2m.x2m./6ft.x6ft.).

Bus

Bus travel presents a different problem. Bikes must be boxed/ bagged for carriage on buses. Greyhound-USA bus stations do not stock bicycle boxes or bags. Ontario Northland and Greyhound Canada bus terminals do stock bike bags. Although the smaller Canadian bus offices may not have the bags.

Lacking a bike bag or box you will have to be creative:

Obtain a bicycle box from a bike shop;

Construct your own box from two or more smaller boxes;

Put your (unboxed) bike into the baggage compartment when the driver's back is turned. Many drivers suddenly disappear with the implication that you should do this heinous crime!

Tandem and long wheel base recumbent bicyclists must check the carrier's rules and regulations. In general these *over size* bicycles can be transported on public transport if they are boxed. Which means more disassembly of the bicycle. A bit of astute questioning and making certain that you receive the answer in writing might prevent problems transporting your bike.

Ah! To be back traveling in Africa (Peace Corps '66-'69) where bikes are simply placed on top of the bus or lashed to the wall of the train's baggage car. How simple! And rarely were the bikes damaged.

How to Box Your Bike

The first time I boxed my bike I did it at home. I inserted extra cardboard into the box to reinforce the long sides of the box. I double sealed all edges using reinforced packing tape. I brought the box to the terminal the day before my departure. It took an interminably long time to do all this packing, >2½ hours. What a chore!

Make life simple for yourself. Pack the box at the terminal. Allow an extra 45 minutes to pack the box. I'm down to 15-20 minutes *bike into box* packing time now!

1. Before you start on your cyclotour take pictures of your bicycle with and without panniers. Open the panniers and take some pictures of the contents of the panniers. If any damage occurs in transit you might need these pictures to assert your claim.

2. Public transit terminals do not have bicycle tools. You will need the following tools (depending on the bolts on your bike.
    Cone wrench (pedals)
    Hex wrenches (brakes, pedals & stem) bolts.
    A roll or two of 2" wide filament reinforced packing tape
    Clothes line (for tying the handlebars to the top tube; and a crank arm to a chain stay).

3. Obtain a bicycle box.

4. Clearly mark the following information on four sides of the bike box. Use a black permanent marker. Write in big letters and numerals.
    Destination:
    Departure date:
    Train, bus or flight number:
    Ticket number:
    Your name:
    ↑ Pointing to the top.

5. Remove both pedals using a cone wrench. The pedals or cranks on new bikes are sometimes removed using a hex wrench. Tape or tie one crank (if not removed) to a chain stay. Put your pedals into one pannier.

6. Loosen the brake cables; loosen the stem; turn the stem or remove it so as to align the handlebars with the top tube. Wrap or tie the handlebars to the top tube or front rack.

6a. If you are transporting your bike on an airplane, reduce your tire pressure by at least half the normal tire pressure. Baggage holds on planes are not usually pressurized and the tube most likely will blow if you don't reduce the pressure.

7. Wheel the bike into the bike box.

8. Secure the bike by wedging your sleeping bag and a pannier

between the bike and the box sides. Do not overload the box with heavy panniers. Carry the other panniers on to the train, plane or bus.

9.   Seal the box with 2" reinforced packing tape.
10. Bring the filled bike box to the baggage room and obtain a baggage claim check. Keep the baggage claim check with you. You will not be able to claim your bike without this claim check.
11. You must use checked baggage for the pannier containing your bicycle tools.

Time needed to prepare your bike and pack the bike box = 20-45 minutes.

At Your Destination
Claim your bicycle!
I have to preface this discussion of damage claims with the fact that my bike has never been damaged traveling via Amtrak and only once on a plane trip. Amtrak stores bikes in an upright position in its baggage cars. Airlines and bus lines store bikes on their side in baggage holds.

Check the exterior of the bicycle box for possible in transit damage. If you see any damage, to the exterior of the bike box, immediately take a picture of the damage and show the damage to the baggage personnel before you open the box.

Open the bike box. Check your bike for any damage or missing items. If damage occurred, immediately show it to the baggage personnel and complete the damage claim form.

After assembling your bike, take a short ride in the terminal to make certain there was no non-visible damage to the gearing, frame, wheels, etc. If you determine that there is some damage, immediately show it to the baggage personnel and take a picture of the damage. Ask for and complete the damage claim form.

Find a local bicycle shop (look in the phone book.) Purchase the part. Copy the receipt and make copies of your completed claim form. Send a copy of the receipt with the original claim form to the carrier. Mail home, the original receipt and one copy of the claim form. It takes 2-6 weeks for most airlines, bus lines or Amtrak to begin to settle baggage damage claims. Enjoy your cyclotour.

Postal Addresses

The proper form of addressing letters is important for your mail to arrive at its destination. The postal systems in both the USA and Canada are very automated. Barcodes are placed automatically on the bottom of envelopes and post cards. Even your handwritten addresses are optical character recognition read.

The clearer you address your letters the faster they speed to their destination. Print! Addresses should be printed in capital letters without punctuation.

Canadian Postal Codes cover a significantly smaller area than US Zip Codes. To conserve space many Postal Codes have been eliminated from the text.

Zip Codes and Postal Codes
> N = Number; L = Letter
> USA Zip Codes consist of five or nine numbers:
> > NNNNN or NNNNN-NNNN
> Canadian Postal codes consist of a combination of two groups of numbers and letters separated by a space.
> > NLN LNL

Use two or three letters to abbreviate terms:
> street = ST; avenue = AVE; road = RD; drive = DR; boulevard = BLVD; *etc.*
> Ontario = ON; Michigan = MI; Ohio = OH; New York = NY; Pennsylvania = PA.

A return address is placed in the upper left corner of the envelope.
The stamp goes on the upper right corner.
The addressee's address is centered on the envelope.
A ½ in. (1.25 cm.) blank space must be left at the bottom of the envelope or post card.

RETURN NAME
ADDRESS   Postage
CITY ST NNNNN

                         NAME
                         ORGANIZATION
                         STREET
                         CITY ST NNNNN
                         NATION

Information Sources

Glossy tourist brochures with all sorts of information and discount coupons will be joyfully supplied by tourist information bureaus. I suggest you write for them.

I have had to search, dig and cajole regional and local planners; transportation agencies; county and municipal officials for valid bicycling route information. A very time consuming and expensive endeavor, which is exactly why you purchased this book! You can simply cyclotour to your heart's mighty beat!

You should request bicycling information if only to make tourism officials aware that people do want to bicycle in their locality. Always request bicycling specific information and local maps. Mention that you obtained the address from *'Round Lake Erie: A Bicyclist's Tour Guide.* It helps!

If you circumnavigate the entire Lake you'll travel through many political units.

Do be careful as you cross a County border. Police may be hiding behind a billboard and if you're speeding, a ticket will be proffered. Passports are not needed when crossing County borders!

Abbreviations used in these listings: TO = Tourism Office; TA = Tourism Association; CVB = Convention & Visitors Bureau; CofC = Chamber of Commerce.

United States Information Sources

Michigan
Travel Michigan, PO Box 26128, Lansing MI 48909, 888 784-7328, http://travel.michigan.org
Monroe County CVB, 106 W. Front St., Ste. C, Monroe MI 48161, 734 457-1030, www.monroeinfo.com
Detroit Metro CVB, 211 W. Fort St., Detroit MI 48226, 313 202-1800, www.visitdetroit.com

New York
New York State Tourism, One Commerce Plz., Albany NY 12245, 518 474-4116, www.iloveny.com
Buffalo Niagara CVB, 617 Main St., Ste. 400, Buffalo NY 14203, 716 852-0511, www.buffalocvb.org
Chautauqua County VB, Chautauqua Institution Welcome Ctr., Rte. 394, PO Box 1441, Chautauqua NY 14722, 800 242-4569, www.tourchautauqua.com

Ohio
Ohio Tourism, PO Box 1001, Columbus OH 43216, 800 282-5393, www.ohiotourism.com
Ashtabula County CVB, 1850 Austinburg Rd., Austinburg OH

44010, 440 275-3202, www.accvb.com

Cleveland (Cuyahoga County) CVB, 50 Public Sq., Ste. 3100 Terminal Tower, Cleveland OH 44113, 216 621-4110, www.travelcleveland.com

Sandusky/Erie County VCB, 4424 Milan Rd. Ste. A, Sandusky OH 44870, 419 625-2984, www.sanduskyohiocedarpoint.com

Lake County VB, 35300 Vine St.-A, Eastlake OH 44095, 440 975-1234, www.lakevisit.com

Lorain County VB, 8025 Leavitt Rd., Amherst OH 44001, 440 984-5282, www.lcvb.org

Greater Toledo (Lucas County) CVB, 401 Jefferson Ave., Toledo OH 43604-1067, 419 321-6404, www.dotoledo.org

Ottawa County VB, 770 S. E. Catawba Rd., Pt. Clinton OH 43452, 419 734-4386, www.lake-erie.com

Sandusky County CVB, 712 North St., Ste. 102, Fremont OH 43420, 419 332-4470, www.sanduskycounty.org

Pennsylvania
Pennsylvania Tourism, www.visitpa.com
Erie Area CVB, 109 Boston Store Pl., Erie PA 16501, 814 454-7191, visiteriepa.com

Canada Information Sources
Ontario Tourism, 10th Fl., Hearst Block, 900 Bay St., Toronto ON M7A 2E1, 800 668-2746, www.ontariotravel.net
Southern Ontario Tourism Org., 180 Greenwich St., Brantford ON N3S 2X6, 519 756-3230, www.soto.on.ca

County Information
Chatham-Kent Tourism, PO Box 944, Chatham ON N7M 5L3, 800 561-6125, www.city.chatham-kent.on.ca
St. Thomas-Elgin TA, 22042 545 Talbot St., St. Thomas ON N5R 6A1, 519 631-8188, www.elgintourist.com
CVB of Windsor, Essex & Pelee Island, 333 Riverside Dr. W., Ste. 103, City Centre, Windsor ON N9A 5K4, 519 255-6530, www.visitwindsor.com
Haldimand Tourism, 45 Munsee St. N., PO Box 400, Cayuga ON N0A 1E0, 905 318-5932, www.tourismhaldimand.com
Niagara Regional Eco & Tourism Corp., 2201 St. David's Rd., PO Box 1042, Thorold ON L2V 4T7, 905 984-3626, www.tourismniagara.com
Norfolk County Tourism, 50 Colborne St., Simcoe ON N3Y 4N5, 519 426-5870, www.norfolktourism.ca

HOW TO READ THE ENTRIES

It's really easy! The entire route is divided into route segments of
~50 mi. (~80 km.)

The route descriptions are written as if you are proceeding
clockwise around either Lake Erie or Georgian Bay.

At the beginning and end of each route section you will see,
besides normal chapter titles, the following barred route
heading:

Cyclotourists traveling **Clockwise** around Lake Erie
read the mileage on the <u>left</u> side of the page
downwards from the top of the page.

⇗

Clockwise	**Port Stanley to**	Counterclockwise
↓ Read mi. (km.)	**Port Colborne**	mi. (km.) Read ↑

⇗

Cyclotourists traveling **Counterclockwise**
read the mileage on the <u>right</u> side of the page
upwards from the bottom of the page.

The first line of an entry gives the cumulative distance in miles
and kilometers (in parentheses) in either direction and a
location intersection. Usually it is in the form of:

17.1 (27.5)   Perry St./OH 163 @ Fulton St.   41.1 (66.1)

Every effort has been made to be accurate in the distances noted.
Mistakes might occur! If so, please send me a post card
noting the error.

The distances are cumulative. You will have to do the subtraction
to find the distances between entries.

The second line of each entry usually gives directions, Turn,
Continue, Stop, Look, *etc.* and where to go. *E. g.*, Turn South
on to Rt. 31. Cardinal compass directions are generally used.
Left and right directions are rarely used.

Turn West on to Perry St./OH 163.

Special Instructions for
Counterclockwise Cyclotourists

Travelers proceeding counterclockwise around Lake Erie are traveling in the <u>opposite</u> way the directions are written. Counterclockwise cyclotourists must **_reverse_** the direction provided in a text entry.

Turn West should be read as:

Turn **East**

This only becomes a problem if you have absolutely no sense of direction. Travelers rapidly get used to reading the mileage (kilometage [*sic*]) on the right side of the page and mentally reversing the directions. Use builds expertise!

Getting lost has always been a treat for me. I've discovered new and interesting routes, places and most importantly people. Think of it as part of the adventure of traveling.

The entries for cities, towns or villages with specific services appears like this:

MARBLEHEAD
Info.:
Cycling & Hiking Info.:
Services & Facilities:
Lodging:
Attractions:

If there is no information then a category does not appear. State and Provincial abbreviations are not included when it is obvious which state or province applies.

Bed & breakfast and campground accommodations listings are complete with addresses and telephone numbers.

Motels are noted simply as *motel* without any other information. For motel accommodations you will have to use a phone book or write to the information source.

Restaurants are listed as, restaurant without a name.

If every bit and piece of information in my files was listed in this *Guide,* it would be more than 700 pages long and weigh over 3 lbs. (1.4 kg.). Thus a bit of research before you depart will allow you to follow the *Less is More* rule!

Of course you could be a *wanderlust* cyclotourist and let your front wheel lead you to wherever!

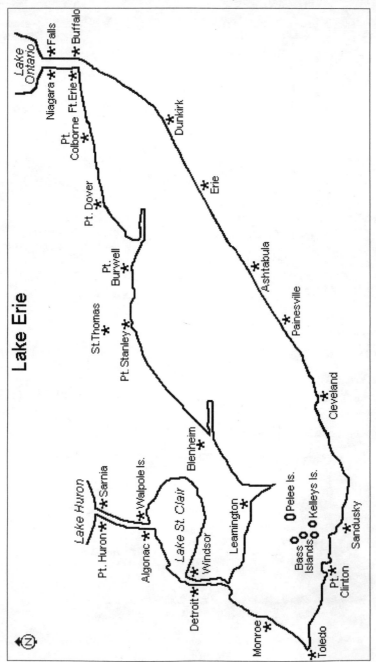

Route Segments			
Segment	Page	Mi.	Km.
Buffalo to Dunkirk , NY	40	50.2	80.0
Dunkirk, NY to Lake City/Girard, PA	50	74.1	119.2
Lake City, PA to Painesville, OH	62	58.2	93.7
Painesville to Cleveland, OH	74	31.9	51.3
Cleveland to Sandusky, OH	82	57.0	91.7
Sandusky to Port Clinton, OH	94	17.6	28.6
Port Clinton to Toledo, OH	102	38.3	61.6
Toledo, OH to River Rouge, MI	106	51.8	83.4
River Rouge to Detroit, MI	112	6.9	11.1
Sub-total: U. S. A. side of Lake Erie		386.0	619.4
Chautauqua Lake Side Trip	58	53.9	86.7
Sub-total: U. S. A. + Chautauqua Rt.		439.9	706.5
Windsor to Malden, ON	118	31.4	50.5
Malden to Leamington/Wheatley	124	36.7	59.1
Wheatley to Dutton	130	66.0	106.2
Dutton to Port Burnwell	134	49.9	80.3
Port Burnwell to Selkirk	138	54.7	88.0
Selkirk to Port Colborne	144	42.3	68.1
Port Colborne to Fort Erie	160	24.0	38.6
Sub-total: Canada side of Lake Erie		305.0	490.8
Welland Canal Route	148	25.8	41.5
Sub-total: Canada + Welland Rt.		330.0	532.3
Total: 'Round Lake Erie circumnavigation only		755.6	1176.5
Total: Including Chautauqua & Welland Rts.		770.5	1238.8

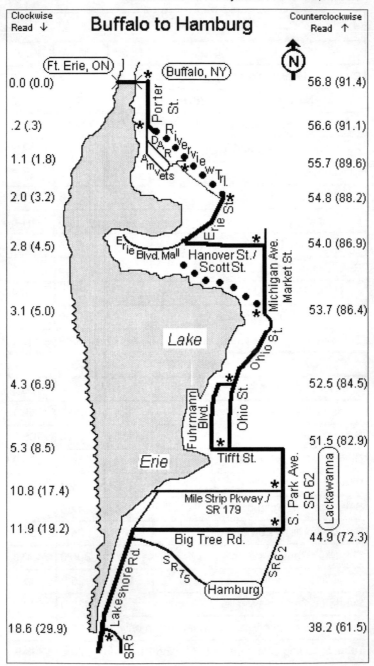

Buffalo to Hamburg

N

Ft. Erie, ON   Buffalo, NY

0.0 (0.0)   56.8 (91.4)

Porter St.

.2 (.3)   56.6 (91.1)

DAR   Riverview

Amvets

1.1 (1.8)   55.7 (89.6)

Trl.

2.0 (3.2)   54.8 (88.2)

Erie St.

Erie Blvd. Mall

2.8 (4.5)   54.0 (86.9)

Hanover St./
Scott St.

Michigan Ave.

Market St.

3.1 (5.0)   53.7 (86.4)

Lake

Ohio St.

4.3 (6.9)   52.5 (84.5)

Fuhrmann Blvd.

Ohio St.

5.3 (8.5)   51.5 (82.9)

Erie   Tifft St.

S. Park Ave.

SR 62

Lackawanna

10.8 (17.4)

Mile Strip Pkway./
SR 179

11.9 (19.2)

Big Tree Rd.   44.9 (72.3)

Lakeshore Rd.

SR 75

SR 62

Hamburg

18.6 (29.9)   38.2 (61.5)

SR 5

PHOENIX RISING ON THE LAKE

To the casual traveler many of the cities along the Lake Erie shore appear to have lost their will to be vibrant cosmopolitan places for people to live and work. Buffalo, like many of the other cities in The Great Lakes area, reached the zenith of its political, economic and social importance sometime between 1890 and 1960.

As industry and population moved from the *Niagara Frontier* to other parts of other nation, and eventually to other nations, the infrastructure and tax base which funded Buffalo's hegemony disappeared. The very reason for a vibrant *waterfront* with shipping activity departed too. The waterfront with its magnificent grain elevators degenerated into a view of what had been rather than what is or will be.

It took 30 years of steady decline and a languishing human spirit before the proverbial phoenix of Buffalo arose to be reestablished just as the buffalo of the Great Plains was reestablished as a viable animal population. For the past decade or so, Buffalo's waterfront has become a place for residents and visitors to enjoy the Lake. Park land now spans the waterfront from the southern edge of the city to its northern edge. Chic housing replaces *project* housing. A waterfront trail leads from the Peace Bridge around the Lake front and north to the Erie Canal at Tonawanda.

In the first edition of this book we stated, "If you return to Buffalo's shore in about five years the River front and Lake front will be more open and inviting." That's what it looks like today.

Clockwise	**Buffalo**	Counterclockwise
Read down ↓	**to Dunkirk**	Read up ↑

0.0 (0.0) Peace Bridge NY Side 56.8 (91.4)
After going through Customs & Immigration, travel straight through the Park to Porter St.
Turn Southwest, towards the River (right), on to Porter St.

BUFFALO

Info: Buffalo Niagara CVB, 617 Main St., Ste. 400, Buffalo NY 14203, 716-852-0511, www.buffalocvb.org AC: 716. ZC: various.
Bicycle info.: Bike shop & camping store downtown near the hostel & CVB; other bike shops, check the phone book. Niagara Frontier Bicycle Club, PO Box 211, 14226, www.nfbc.com. WNY Mountain Bicycling Assn. (WNYMBA) www.wnymba.org. Buffalo bike info: www.gbrfc.org; www.bluemoon.net/~skibby.

Services: All. Hospitals, colleges. Peace Bridge, 884-6752.
Public Transportation: Buffalo is a major transportation center.
Airport: The airport is 7.8 mi (12.5 km.) East of the Peace Bridge
on NY 33/Genesee St.   NY 33 is a busy heavily trafficked street
which goes through industrial areas. But it is straight and direct to
the airport.
Bus: Intercity buses stop at the Transportation Ctr., Ellicott &
Division Sts. Greyhound, 855-7531; Trailways, 852-1750.
City & suburban buses: An extensive system of buses & light rail
transit is provided by the NFTA, Transportation Ctr., Ellicott &
Division Sts., 14203, 855-7211. All buses have bike racks. Metro
buses go to North to Niagara Falls; East to Lockport (Erie Canal);
& South to Hamburg. Check the schedules as service is limited to
suburban & rural areas.
Railroad: Baggage service on Amtrak trains is a necessity for
bicyclists. The downtown Buffalo-Exchange St. station (856-2075)
does not have baggage service. The Buffalo-Depew station (683-
8440) does have baggage service for the *Lake Shore Express.*
To the Peace Bridge from the Buffalo-Depew Amtrak station: Ask
someone how to get to Walden Ave. It's actually in front of the rail
terminal but obscured by a shopping mall.   Travel West on
Waldon Ave. for 5.8 mi. (9.4 km.) to Genesee St./NY 33. Turn
Southwest on to Genesee St. Genesee St. ends at City Hall/
Niagara Sq. Go across the Sq. to Niagara St./NY 266 & follow the
signs to the Bridge.
Attractions: Many street festivals.
Architecture: Art Deco buildings downtown.
Museums: Albright-Knox Art Gallery, 1285 Elmwood Ave., 882-
8700; Mus. of Science, 1020 Humboldt Pkwy., 896-5200; Zoo,
300 Parkside Ave., 837-3900; Botanical Gardens, 2655 S. Park
Ave., 696-3555; Buffalo & Erie Co. Hist. Soc., 25 Nottingham Ct.,
873-9644; Naval & Servicemen's Pk., 1 Naval Pk. Cove, 847-
1773; Theodore Roosevelt Nat'l Hist. Site, 641 Delaware Ave.,
884-0095.
Music & Theater: Buffalo Philharmonic Orchestra, 71 Symphony
Cir., 885-5000. On Main St., in downtown, are a series of restored
theaters, check the newspaper for current shows.
Sports: Bisons baseball, 846-2003; Bills football (summer camp in
Rochester, NY), Sabers hockey, Bandits lacrosse.
Nature: Tifft Nature Pres., 1200 Fuhrmann Blvd., 825-6397.
Lodging: Motels are downtown. Buffalo HI Hostel, 667 Main St.,
852-5222. B&Bs: Beau Fleuve, 242 Linwood Ave., 882-6116;
Betty's, 398 Jersey St., 881-0700; Richmond Place Inn, 45
Richmond Ave., 881-3242.

0.0 (0.0)   Peace Bridge NY Side   56.8 (91.4)
After going through Customs & Immigration, travel
straight through the Park to Porter St.   Turn
Southwest, towards the River (right), on to Porter St.
          Customs & Immigration
To enter the USA 2 forms of picture identification are
needed. A driver's license or police photo id and,
preferably, a passport. Be prepared! Have a copy of your
equipment list ready to present to the customs officer.
To enter Canada, 2 forms of picture identification are
needed.
The customs and immigration rules are constantly being
revised.
Counterclockwise cyclists note: walk your bicycle on the
Peace Bridge walkway rather than riding on the bridge's
roadway. Peace Bridge tel.: 884-6752.

0.2 (0.3)   Porter St.   56.6 (91.1)
          @ LaSalle Pk. Niagara R./Riverwalk Trail
The entrance to the Riverwalk Trail is about a wheel's
diameter before the entrance to LaSalle Park. It may be
obscured by vegetation. If you use the trail then skip to
2.0 (3.2)   Riverwalk Trail @ Erie St.   54.8 (88.2)

If you can not find the Riverwalk Trail head, use the
following directions to Erie St.
Enter LaSalle Pk. Travel straight to the River. At the
River, turn South on to the Amvets Dr. or the sidewalk
bordering the shore. The sidewalk/trail along the shore
line is not marked well but it is obvious.

1.1 (1.8)   Riverwalk Trail   55.7 (89.6)
          @ South End of LaSalle Pk.
Follow the Trail markers and signs inland to the Riverwalk Trail which winds behind the condominiums at this
point. It emerges a bit further South on to the River's
shore and brings you to Erie St. near the Naval Museum.

2.0 (3.2)   Riverwalk Trail @ Erie St.   54.8 (88.2)
If you took the Riverwalk Trail all the way from Porter St.
to this point then turn Southwest (towards the River &
away from the overhead highway) on to Erie St.
If you followed the shore line then continue traveling
South.
Counterclockwise cyclists: you will be able to follow the
Trail all the way to Porter St. The Trail head at this end of
the Riverwalk Trail is clearly signed near the RR tracks.

Follow the Trail behind Lakeshore Condo development; the trail parallels the trolley line. This off-road Trail ends at Porter St. near the Peace Bridge.

2.2 (3.5)   River/Hanover St. @ Erie St.   54.6 (87.9)
If you're on the Niagara River shore line, skip this entry.
folks who took the Riverwalk Trail directly from Porter St.:
As you cross Hanover St. you'll once again see the Riverfront Trail along the River shore. Begin riding on this shore line section of the Riverwalk Trail.
Alternatively turn South on to Hanover St. and continue to Buffalo Naval Pk. Going straight at this intersection brings you on to Erie Mall Blvd., into Marina Pk. and the lighthouse.

2.4 (3.9)   Hanover St./Scott St.   54.4 (87.5)
                   @ Commercial St..
                   River @ Naval & Serviceman's Museum
Visit the Museum then Turn East on To Hanover St./ Scott St. Hanover changes its name to Scott St. after 1 block. Eventually, 5 years from now, there might be an off road trail or signed on road trail from this point South.

2.8 (4.5)   Scott St. @ Michigan Ave.   54.0 (86.9)
Turn South on to Michigan Ave. (old name Maple St.)

3.1 (5.0)   Michigan Ave. @ Ohio St.   53.7 (86.4)
Turn South on to Ohio St.

4.3 (6.9)   Ohio St. @ One Way division   52.5 (84.5)
Turn West, towards the Lake; go under the overpass on to Fuhrman Blvd.

5.3 (8.5)   Fuhrman Blvd. @ Tifft St.   51.5 (82.9)
Turn East on to Tifft St. Fuhrman Blvd. becomes a discontinuous road along the shore. A trail along the shore is being planned and developed.
Counterclockwise travelers turn North on to Fuhrman Blvd./Ohio St. Follow the signs to Tifft Nature Pres. & continue northwards. Tifft Farm Nature Preserve.

7.0 (11.3)   Tifft St. @ South Park/NY 62   49.8 (80.1)
Turn South on to NY 62/South Park Ave. LACKAWANNA

8.3 (13.4)   South Park St./NY 62   48.5 (78.1)
                   @ Ridge Rd.
Continue travelling South on NY 62.

Hamburg to Dunkirk

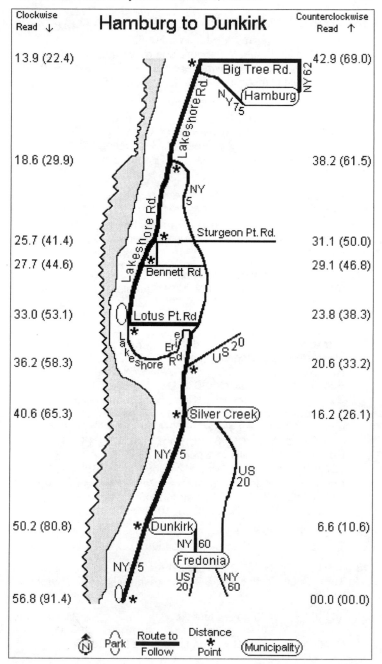

Clockwise Read ↓		Counterclockwise Read ↑
13.9 (22.4)	Big Tree Rd. / Hamburg / NY 62 / NY 75 / Lakeshore Rd.	42.9 (69.0)
18.6 (29.9)	NY 5	38.2 (61.5)
25.7 (41.4)	Sturgeon Pt. Rd. / Lakeshore Rd.	31.1 (50.0)
27.7 (44.6)	Bennett Rd.	29.1 (46.8)
33.0 (53.1)	Lotus Pt. Rd.	23.8 (38.3)
36.2 (58.3)	Lakeshore Rd. / Erie Rd. / US 20	20.6 (33.2)
40.6 (65.3)	Silver Creek	16.2 (26.1)
	NY 5 / US 20	
50.2 (80.8)	Dunkirk / NY 60 / Fredonia	6.6 (10.6)
56.8 (91.4)	NY 5 / US 20 / NY 60	00.0 (00.0)

Legend:
- N (north)
- Park
- Route to Follow
- Distance * Point
- Municipality

10.8 (17.4)　　　　Mile Strip Expwy./NY 179　　　　43.8 (70.5)
　　　　　　　　　　@ South Park Ave./NY 62
It is possible to turn West here and go towards the River.
At the River is Woodlawn Beach St. Pk., 716 826-1930,
the nearest campground to Buffalo. BLASDELL.

11.9 (19.2)　　　　South Park St./NY 62　　　　44.9 (72.3)
　　　　　　　　　　@ Big Tree Rd.
Turn West towards the Lake.
Turning East on to Big Tree Rd. & traveling for 4.4 mi.
(7.0 km.) will bring you to Orchard Park & East Aurora.

HAMBURG

Info.: Hamburg CofC, PO Box 460, 1 Centennial Park,
Hamburg NY 14075, 716 649-7917. AC: 716. ZC: 14075.
Attraction: Buffalo Raceway Harness Racing, 649-1280
Lodging: Motels. B&B: Colonel's Retreat, 222 Pierce
Ave., 648-1880.

ORCHARD PARK & EAST AURORA

Info: Orchard Park CofC, 4211 Buffalo Rd. Ste. 14,
Orchard Park NY 14127, 589-7004. Greater East Aurora
CofC, 431 Main St., East Aurora NY 14052, 652-8444.
AC: 716.
Attractions: Orchard Park: Of particular interest to
bicyclists is the Pedaling History Mus., 3942 N. Buffalo
Rd. (Rts. 240/277), 662-3853. Well worth the diversion.
Buffalo Bills Football, One Bills Dr., 648-1800.
East Aurora: Aurora Hist. Soc., 57 Shearer Ave., 655-
0571; Elbert Hubbard Roycroft Mus. (Arts & Crafts Move-
ment), 363 Oakwood Ave., 652-4735; Toy Town Mus.,
606 Girard Ave., 655-3888; Knox Farm St., Pk., Knox
Rd., 652-2207; Holland Speedway, 2 N. Main St., 537-
2272; Millard Fillmore House, 24 Shearer St., 652-3280.
Lodging: Motels. East Aurora: Parkedge Farm, 140
Gypsy Ln., 652-5600; Roycroft Inn, 48 S. Grove St., 652-
5552; Wm. Warren Homestead, 107 Pine St., 655-1476.

13.9 (22.4)　　　　Big Tree Rd./NY 5　　　　42.9 (69.0)
Turn South on to NY 5. Athol Springs

18.6 (29.9)　　　　NY 5 @ Old Lakeshore Rd.,　　　　38.2 (61.5)
Turn Southwest on to Old Lakeshore.Rd. Pinehurst
Village

25.7 (41.4)　　　　Old Lakeshore Rd.　　　　31.1 (50.0)
　　　　　　　　　　@ Sturgeon Pt. Rd.
Continue travelling South on Lakeshore Rd./Dennis Rd.

[Note: Just past Wendt Beach Pk/, Lakeshore bears Southwest, towards the lake; if you miss the turn off, continue South on Dennis Rd.
Attraction: In Eden, 6 mi. (10 km.) East along Sturgeon Pt. Rd. is the Original American Kazoo Factory & Mus., 8703 S. Main St., 992-3960.

27.2 (43.8)   Dennis Rd. @ Bennett Rd.]   29.6 (47.6)
Turn West on to Bennett Rd.]

27.7 (44.6)   Bennett Rd.   29.1 (46.8)
                  @ Lakeshore Rd.
Turn South on to Lakeshore Rd.
ANGOLA: **Info:** Evans Town, 8787 Erie Rd., Angola NY 14006, 549-5547. AC: 716.
Lodging: Motel. Camping: Evangola St. Pk., 549-1760; Point Breeze Camp, 9456 Lake Shore Rd., 549-3768.

32.0 (51.5)   Lakeshore Rd. @ Park Rd.   24.8 (39.9)
Entrance to Evangola St. Pk., 543-1760.

33.0 (53.1)   Lakeshore Rd. @ Lotus Pt. Rd.   23.8 (38.3)
Turn East on to Lotus Pt. Rd.

34.4 (55.4)   Lotus Pt. Rd. @ NY 5   22.4 (36.0)
Turn South on to NY 5.

36.2 (58.3)   NY 5 Jct. US 20   20.6 (33.2)
Northern junction; Continue riding South on NY 5; US 20 is a winery route but has more traffic than NY 5. SILVER CREEK: **Info:** Silver Creek Village, 172 Central Ave., Silver Creek NY 14136, 716 934-3240. **Attractions:** There are many wineries between **Lodging:** Pinewoods Cottage B&B, 11634 York Rd., 716 934-4173.

40.6 (65.3)   NY 5 Jct. US 20   16.2 (26.1)
Southern junction; Continue South on NY 5. Silver Creek

50.2 (80.8)   Central Ave. @ NY 5   6.6 (10.6)
Continue South on NY 5. Turning towards the Lake brings you on to the pier.

DUNKIRK

Info.: Chautauqua County CofC, 212 Lake Shore Dr. W., Dunkirk NY 14048, 716 366-6200, AC: 716. ZC: 14048
Services: All. Hospital.
Attractions: Dunkirk Lighthouse, 1 Lighthouse Dr., 366-5050; Dunkirk Hist. Soc., 513 Washington Ave., 366-3797; Woodbury Vineyard, 3230 S. Roberts Rd., 679-9463.

Lodging: Motels. Camping: Lake Erie St. Pk., NY 5, (7 miles West of Dunkirk), Dunkirk NY 14048, 792-9214.

FREDONIA

Info: Fredonia: Fredonia CofC, 5 E. Main St., Fredonia NY 14063, 716 679-1565. AC 716. ZC: 14063.
Services: Bike shop
Attraction: Darwin R. Barker Hist. Mus., 20 E. Main St., 672-2314
Lodging: Motels. Brookside Manor B&B, 3728 NY 83, 672-7721; The White Inn, 52 East Main St., 672-2103.

56.8 (91.4)   Lake Erie State Park @ NY 5   0.0 (0.0)
Lake Erie St. Pk., NY 5, (7 miles West of Dunkirk), Dunkirk NY 14048, 792-9214.

Clockwise	**Dunkirk to**	Counterclockwise
Read down ↓	**Buffalo**	Read up ↑

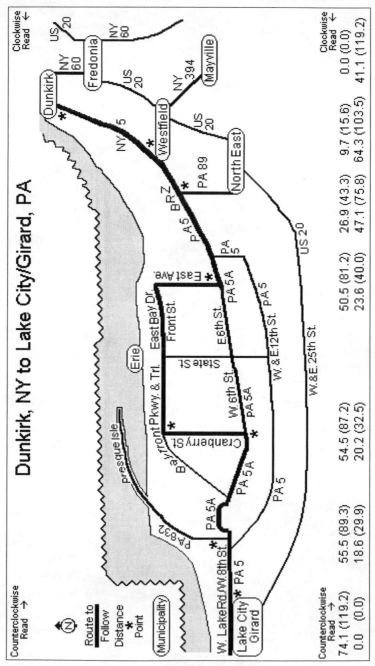

Dunkirk, NY to Lake City/Girard, PA

INTELLECTUAL REVIVALISM

During the late 19th Century The Great Lakes were the *in* place for vacationing upper middle and upper class families. Here, the relatively wealthy had summer homes on the shore or on one of the numerous feeder lakes which were part of the enormous Great Lakes Basin. To amuse themselves the wealthy raced yachts; played tennis; and supported the local economy.

For the middle class there were secular and religious summer camps for children and adults. These were places where lower management personnel and factory workers could escape the rigors of the industrial revolution. It was a country atmosphere where their children could breathe fresh air and learn about the non-urban environment.

Organizations, which operated these summer programs, had ulterior motives. By attending these summer retreats the organizations' hoped that their members would learn, practice and more readily adhere to their philosophy. Most of the more secular camps simply wanted their participants to have a good time, an enjoyable vacation.

Most of the lower cost camps were operated by religious or political organizations. For the moderate cost of room and board adults and children were taught the values of the organization usually in pleasant surroundings and in a fun rather than schooling atmosphere.

This is not as sinister as it sounds. The participating *campers* were not coerced to come to summer camp, they came voluntarily to *get away from* the city and to be more committed to the organizations' values. Most adult *camps* were begun and operated by religious institutions for training adult lay leaders. Many of these summer escapes tried to uplift the intellect as well as the rote spirituality of their adherents. Over the course of time the more fundamentalist (religious & political) of the adult summer camps incorporated more cosmopolitan and sophisticated programs to attract and finance their more provincial values laden programs. The most successful of these camps is the Chautauqua Institution, which began as a Methodist Church summer program for training adult leaders.

Now the Institution has a full complement of secular intellectual programs to complement the Methodist programs. It is these intellectual programs which has made Chautauqua a national symbol for thoughtful discourse about national, foreign ethical and intellectual ideas.

Clockwise	**Dunkirk, NY**	Counterclockwise
Read down ↓	**to Lake City/Girard PA**	Read up ↑

0.0 (0.0)   Lake Erie St. Park @ NY 5   74.1 (119.2)
Turn Southwest on to NY 5.
Lake Erie St. Pk., NY 5, (7 miles West of Dunkirk),
Dunkirk NY 14048, 792-9214.

9.7 (15.6)   NY 5 @ NY 394   64.3 (103.5)
                   Barcelona/Westfield
Continue travelling South on NY 5.
Barcelona: Lighthouse & park on the Lake.

WESTFIELD

Info: Westfield CofC, PO Box 25, Westfield NY 14787,
326-4000. ZC: 14767. AC: 716.
Services: All.
Attraction: Chautauqua Hist. Soc., NY 394 & US 20,
326-2977 (see side trip); Johnson Estate Winery, W.
Main Rd., US 20, 326-2191; Vetter Vineyards, E. Main
Rd., 326-3100.
Lodging: B&Bs: Brewer House, 112 E. Main St., 326-
3415; Candlelight Lodge, 143 E. Main St., 326-2830;.
Lakeside, 8223 East Lake Rd., 326-3757; Sugar Shack,
7218 NY 5, 326-3351.
The William Seward Inn, 6645 S. Portage Rd., 326-4151;
Westfield House, East Main Rd., 326-6262. Camping:
Blue Water Beach Cpgd., 7364 E. Lake Rd., 326-3540;
Brookside Beach Cpgd., PO Box 130, NY 5, 326-3096;
Westfield/Lake Erie KOA, 8001 NY 5, 326-3573.

16.9 (27.2)   NY 76 @ NY 5   57.1 (91.9)
Continue traveling on NY 5. The NY-PA border is about
2.5 mi. (4 km.) from here, continue travelling South on
PA 5 at the border.

RIPLEY

Info: Ripley CofC, PO Box 366, Ripley NY 14775. 716
736-2211. ZC: 14775. AC: 716. Ripley is about 1.5 mi.
(2.4 km.) South of this intersection.
Bike Info.: As you cross into PA you will notice signs for
PA Bike Route Z. This route generally follows the Lake
Erie shore.
Attraction: Schloss Doepken Winery, 9177 Old NY 20,
326-3636.
Lodging: Lakeside Cpgd., NY 5 at Pa. line, 736-3362.

26.9 (43.3)   PA 89 @ PA 5   47.1 (75.8)
Continue travelling on PA 5.

NORTH EAST

Info: North East CofC, PO Box 466; North East PA 16428, 814 725-4262. ZC: 16428. AC: 814.
Bike Info.: Bike shop.
Attractions: Hornby School Mus., 10000 Cott Station Rd., 739-2720; Lake Shore Railway Mus., 31 Wall St., 725-1911; North East Mus., 25 Vine St., 899-6022; Heritage Wine Cellars, 12162 E. Main Rd., 725-8015; Mazza Vineyards, 11815 East Lake Rd., 725-8695; Penn Shore Winery, 10225 East Lake Rd., 725-8688; Presque Isle Wine Cellars, 9440 W. Main Rd., 725-1314; Arrowhead Wine Cellars, 12073 E. Main Rd., 725-5509. Lake Erie Speedway, 10700 Delmas Dr., 878-5553.
Lodging: B&B: Grape Arbor Inn, 51 E. Main St., 725-5522; Vineyard, 10757 Sidehill Rd., 725-8998. Camping: Creekside Cpgd., 10834 NY 89, 725-5523; Family Affair Cpgd., 9460 Findley Lake Rd., 725-8112.

40.5 (65.2)   Shubs Beach Pk.   33.6 (54.1)
@ PA 5/E. Lake Rd.
Continue travelling on PA 5. Nice place to stop.

48.0 (77.2)   PA 5Jct. PA 5A   26.1 (42.0)
Travel West on PA 5A/6th St.
PA 5 traverses the southern edge of Erie.

50.5 (81.2)   East Ave. @ PA 5A   23.6 (40.0)
Turn North (towards the Lake). A sign may say "to Bayfront Pkwy./Front St."
Alternatively, continue traveling on PA 5A/E. 6th St. which goes through the center of the business district.

50.9 (81.9)   East Bay Dr. @ East Ave.   23.2 (37.3)
Turn West on to East Bay Dr.

51.3 (82.5)   East Bay Rd.   22.8 (36.7)
@ Bayfront Pkwy./Trail/Front St.
Continue westward along Front St. or the Trail which parallels Bayfront Pkwy.

52.3 (84.1)   State St. @ Bayfront Trail   21.8 (35.0)
Continue on the Trail. Landmark: Bicentennial Tower.
Turn South on to State St. to go into the center of Erie and to PA 5A.

ERIE

Info: Erie Area CVB, 100 Boston Store Pl.; Erie PA 16501, 814 454-7191. ZC: various. AC: 814.

Bike info: Bike shop. Clubs: Lakeside Bicycle Assn., PO Box 10751, Erie PA 16414. 455-6512; Frontier Bike Club, 1712 W. 8th St., Erie PA 16505, 814 456-0803.

Services: All. Erie Metro Transit Auth., 127 E 14th St., 459-3515, all buses have bike racks. Amtrak, Greyhound, Erie Airport, 4411 W. 12th St., 833-4258.

Attractions: Nature: Asbury Woods Nature Ctr., 4105 Asbury Rd., 835-5356; Lake Erie Arboretum, 1650 Norcross Rd., 825-1700; Presque Isle St. Pk., PO Box 8510, 833-7424.

Museums: Erie Maritime Mus. & US Niagara, 150 E. Front St., 452-2744; Erie Art Mus., 411 State St., 459-5477; Erie Planetarium, 356 W. 6th St., 871-5790; Erie Zoo, 423 W. 38th St., 864-4091; expERIEnce Children's Mus., 420 French St., 453-3743; Firefighters Hist. Mus., 428 Chestnut St., 456-5969; Pennsylvania Aquarium,1006 State St., Erie Co. Hist. Soc., 419 State St., 454-1813; Lawrence Pk. Hist. Soc. Mus., 4230 Iroquois Ave., 899-7119; Marx Toy Mus., 50 E. Bloomfield Pkwy., 825-6500; Land Lighthouse,6th St. at Lake. Sports: Seawolves Soccer, 110 E. 10 St., 456-1300; Sailors Baseball, ,Ainsworth Field, 453-3900; Erie Downs, 7700 Peach St., 866-3678. Also, Erie Wave Basketball, 456-9283; Otters Hockey, 455-7779.

Lodging: Motels. B&Bs: Boothby Inn, 311 West 6th St., 456-1888; Spencer House, 519 W. 6th St., 454-5984; Camping: Cassidy's Presque Isle Trailer Pk., 3749 Zimmerly Rd., 833-6035; Moon Meadows, 9915 Station Rd., 725-9360; Sara Coyne Cpgd., 50 Peninsula Dr., 833-4560.

53.6 (86.2)   Liberty Pk.@ Bayfront Trail   20.5 (33.0)
Continue traveling on the Trail or through the *Park &
Ride* parking lot.
Look for a traffic light and head towards it. Do not
attempt to cross Bayfront Pkwy. except at the light.
Follow the Trail signs to PA 5A. The Trail may end at
this point. It is still being constructed at the time of
publication. If so you may have to ride on busy Bayfront
Pkwy. to Cranberry St. or to PA 5A/W. 6th St.

54.5 (87.2)   Cranberry St. @ Bayfront Trl.   19.9 (32.0)
Traffic light at Cranberry Dr. & Bayfront Pkwy.
Cross Bayfront Pkwy. only at this traffic light.
Turn South on to Cranberry St.

54.7 (88.0)   PA 5A/W. 6th St.   20.2 (32.5)
                     @ Cranberry St.
Turn West on to PA 5A/West 8th St.
Counterclockwise cyclotourists can continue traveling
East on PA 5A/W. 8th St. rather than using the Lake
front route.

53.4 (85.9)   Bayfront Pkwy. @ 6th St./PA 5A   20.7 (33.3)
Continue travelling on PA 5A/Cherokee Dr.
Cherokee Dr. forms a semi-circle around Frontier Pk.
connecting W. 6th St. with W. 8th St.

53.9 (86.7)   W 8th St. @ Cherokee Dr./PA 5A   20.2 (32.5)
Continue travelling on PA 5A.

55.5 (89.3)   PA 832/Peninsula Dr.   18.6 (29.9)
                     @ W. 8th St./PA 5A
Turn North towards the Lake on to Peninsula Dr./PA
832 to go to Presque Isle St. Pk. (no camping).
Presque Isle St. Park is a wonderful place to bike. It
has beautiful clean sandy beaches & great birding.
Motels (inexpensive) and campgrounds are on PA 5A &
near the Park's entrance.
Continue straight on PA 5A/W. 8th St.

58.3 (93.8)   PA 5/W. 12th St.   15.8 (25.4)
                     Jct. PA 5A/W. Lake Rd.
Follow PA 5 westward.

66.8 (107.5)   Avonia Rd./PA 98 @ PA 5 Avonia   7.3 (11.7)
Continue Southwest on PA 5.
FAIRVIEW: is about 2.5 mi. (4 km.) South. ZC: 16415.
AC: 814.

Attraction: Sturgeon House, 4302 Garwood St., 474-5855.
Lodging: Camping: It is at least 7 mi. (11 km.) to these 2 cpgds. Hills Family Cpgd., 6300 Sterrettania Rd. (PA 832), 833-3272; R K Cpgd, 6601 Sterrettania Rd., 833-0611.

74.1 (119.2)   N. Lake Rd. @ PA 5/W. Lake Rd.   0.0 (0.0)
Continue travelling on PA 5.

LAKE CITY - GIRARD

Info: Girard/Lake City Area CofC, PO Box 118, Lake City PA 16423, 814 774-3535. Girard: ZC: 16417. Lake City ZC: 16423. AC: 814.
Attractions: Battles Mus. of Rural Life, 436 Walnut St., 774-4788; Gudgeonville Bridge (4 mi. S), Gudgeonville Rd., Hazel Kibler Mus., 522 E. Main St., 774-4168.
Lodging: Motels. B&B: Gunnison House, 159 Main St. E., Girard, 774-5550. Camping: Folly's End Cpgd., PA 98, Girard, 474-5730; Camp Eriez, 9356 W. Lake Rd, Lake City, 774-8381. Virginia's Beach Cpgd. (about 5 mi. (8 km.) West of Girard), 352 Holiday Rd., North Springfield PA 16430, 814 922-3261.

Clockwise	**Lake City/Girard, PA**	Counterclockwise
Read down ↓	**to Dunkirk, NY**	Read up ↑

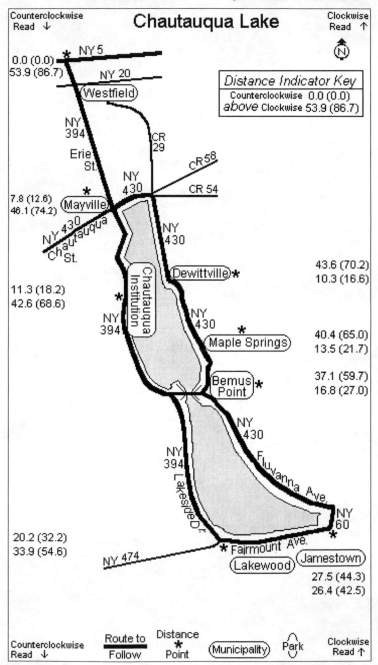

Chautauqua Lake

Counterclockwise Read ↓

Clockwise Read ↑

N

NY 5

0.0 (0.0)
53.9 (86.7)

NY 20

Westfield

Distance Indicator Key
Counterclockwise 0.0 (0.0)
above Clockwise 53.9 (86.7)

NY 394

Erie St.

CR 29

CR 58

NY 430

CR 54

7.8 (12.6)
46.1 (74.2)
Mayville

NY 430

Chautauqua

NY 430

Chautauqua St.

Dewittville

43.6 (70.2)
10.3 (16.6)

11.3 (18.2)
42.6 (68.6)

Chautauqua Institution

NY 394

NY 430

Maple Springs

40.4 (65.0)
13.5 (21.7)

Bemus Point

37.1 (59.7)
16.8 (27.0)

NY 430

NY 394

Fluvanna Ave.

Lakeside Dr.

NY 60

20.2 (32.2)
33.9 (54.6)

NY 474

Fairmount Ave.

Lakewood

Jamestown

27.5 (44.3)
26.4 (42.5)

Counterclockwise Read ↓

<u>Route to</u> Follow

Distance * Point

Municipality

Park

Clockwise Read ↑

Counterclockwise	**Chautauqua Lake Route**	Clockwise
Read down ↓	**Round the Lake**	Read up ↑

0.0 (0.0)   NY 5 @ NY 394   53.9 (86.7)
Turn South on to NY 394.

1.6 (2.6)   US 20 @ NY 394   52.3 (84.2)
Continue travelling on NY 394.

WESTFIELD

Info: Westfield CofC, PO Box 25, Westfield NY 14787, 326-4000. ZC: 14767. AC: 716.
Attraction: Chatauqua Hist. Soc., NY 394 & US 20, 326-2977; Johnson Estate Winery, W. Main Rd., US 20, 326-2191; Vetter Vineyards, E. Main Rd.., 326-3100;
Lodging: B&Bs: Brewer House, 112 E. Main St., 326-3415; Candlelight Lodge, 143 E. Main St., 326-2830;.
Lakeside, 8223 East Lake Rd., 326-3757; Sugar Shack, 7218 NY 5, 326-3351;
The William Seward Inn, 6645 S. Portage Rd., 326-4151; Westfield House, East Main Rd., 326-6262. Camping: Blue Water Beach Cpgrd., 7364 E. Lake Rd., 326-3540; Brookside Beach Cpgd., PO Box 130, NY 5, 326-3096; Westfield/Lake Erie KOA, 8001 NY 5, 326-3573.

7.8 (12.6)   NY 430/Chautauqua St.   46.1 (74.2)
               @ NY 394 Erie St.
Continue on NY 394/Chautauqua St.

MAYVILLE

Info: Chatauqua County CVB, 4 N. Erie St., Mayville NY 14757, 716 753-4304. ZC: 14757. AC: 716.
Lodging: B&Bs: Farmington Inn, 6642 East Lake Rd., 753-7989; Stuart Manor, 4351 West Lake Rd., 789-9902; Village Inn, 111 S. Erie St., 753-3583. Camping: Camp Prendergast, 6238 Davis Rd., 789-3485; Chautauqua Family Cpgrd., PO Box 194, Dinsbier Rd., 753-2212.

8.5 (13.7)   Water St./NY 394   45.4 (73.1)
               @ Erie St./NY 394
Continue on NY 394.

8.7 (14.0)   Lake Rd./NY 394 @ Water St.   45.2 (72.7)
Continue on NY 394/Lake Rd.

11.3 (18.2)   Chautauqua Institution   42.6 (68.6)
@ Lake Rd./NY 394
Yeah! It's the same, continue on Lake Rd.

CHAUTAUQUA

Info: Chautauqua County Visitors Bureau, PO Box 1441, Chautauqua NY 14722, 800 242-4569.
ZC: 14722. AC: 716.
Attraction: Chautauqua Institution, 1 Ames St., Box 1095, 357-6200/357-6250.
Lodging: B&Bs: Carey Cottage Inn, 9 Bowman Ave., 357-2245; Heather's Inn, 4 Bowman Ave., 357-4804: Brasted House, 4833 West Lake Ave., 753-5500; Englewood Guest House, PO Box 42, 357-3300; Summer House Inn, 22 Peck, 357-2101; The Ashland, 10 Vincent, 357-2257; The Cambridge Inn, 9 Roberts St.,357-3292; The Maple Inn, Bowman at Wythe, 357-4583; The Vera, 25 S. Terrace, 357-2257.
DEWITTSVILLE: Camping: Chautauqua Heights Cpgd., 5652 Thumb Rd., Dewittville 14728, 386-3804.

20.0 (32.2)   CR 43 @ Lake Rd./NY 394   33.9 (54.6)
Follow NY 394/Lakeside Dr. CR 43 goes to Ashville. Ashville, ZC: 14710. AC: 716. **Lodging:** B&B: Chestnut Hill on the Lake, 3736 Victoria Rd., 789-5371; Hemlock Hollow, 5901 Stow Rd., 789-9143.

23.7 (38.1)   Shadyside Rd./NY 474   30.2 (48.6)
@ Fairmount Ave./NY 394
Follow Fairmont Ave./NY 394 through Lakewood.
Traveling West on NY 474 will bring you to Panama.
Attraction: Great Blue Heron Music Fest., 2361 Wait Corners Rd., 761-6184, Panama Rocks Scenic Park, 11 Rock Hill Rd., 782-2845.

27.5 (44.3)   Main St./NY 60   26.4 (42.5)
@ Fairmount Ave./NY 394
Turn North on to NY 60/Main St. NY 60 follows a diagonal route to Fredonia.

JAMESTOWN

Info: Chautauqua CC, 101 W. 5th St., Jamestown NY 14701, 716 484-1101. Bike info.: Jamestown Cycle Shop, 10 Harrison St., 664-4112. ZC: 14701. AC: 716.
Attraction: Luci-Desi Museum, 212 Pine St., 484-7070; Roger Tory Peterson Natural Hist. Inst., 311 Curtis St., 665-2473; The Lucille Ball-Desi Arnaz Ctr., 100 E. 3rd

St., 484-0800; Jamestown Audubon Nature Ctr., 1600
Riverside Rd., 569-2345.
Lodging: B&Bs: Partridge Sheldon Mansion, 70
Prospect St., 484-2350, Camping: Hidden Valley, 299
Kiantone Rd., 569-5433; Top-A-Rise Cpgd., 4267 Dean
School Rd., Falconer, NY 14733, 287-3222.

28.2 (45.4)   NY 430/Fluvanna Ave.   25.7 (41.4)
                     @ NY 60/Main St.
Turn Northwest on to NY 430/Fluvanna Ave.

37.1 (59.7)   Lakeside Dr. @ Main St./NY 430   16.8 (27.0)
Turn East on to Lakeside Dr. Follow Lakeside Dr. along
the shore rather than NY 430. NY 430 junctions with NY
17 and becomes a limited access fast moving road.
BEMUS POINT: ZC: 14712. AC: 716. **Attractions:**
Gerry Rodeo, PO Box 182, Gerry NY 14740 (~10 mi. E.
of Bemus Pt.), 716 985-4847. **Lodging:** B&B: Country
House, 4836 Hale Rd., 753-7989. Camping: Wildwood
Acres, 5006 Brown Rd., 386-7037.

39.7 (63.9)   NY 430 @ Lakeside Dr.   14.2 (22.9)
Turn North on to NY 430 just after Sunset Bay

40.4 (65.0)   Miller Hill Rd. @ NY 430   13.5 (21.7)
Continue on NY 430.
MAPLE SPRINGS: **Attraction:** Midway Park, NY 430,
386-3165. **Lodging**: B&B: Lake Side Inn, 4696
Chautauqua Ave., 386-2500.

43.6 (70.2)   CR 37/Wright Rd. @ NY 430   10.3 (16.6)
Continue on NY 430.
DEWITTVILLE: **Lodging:** Chautauqua Heights Cpgd.,
5652 Thumb Rd., 386-3804.

46.1 (74.2)   NY 394/Erie St.   7.8 (12.6)
                     @ NY 430/Chautauqua St.
Turn North on to NY 394/Erie St.

52.3 (84.2)   NY 20 @ NY 394   1.6 (2.6)
Continue travelling North on NY 394. WESTFIELD

53.9 (86.7)   NY 5 @ NY 394   0.0 (0.0)
Clockwise Lake Erie travelers turn West on to NY 5.
Counterclockwise Lake Erie rounders turn East on NY 5.

Counterclockwise	**Chautauqua Lake Route**	Clockwise
Read down ↓	**Round the Lake**	Read up ↑

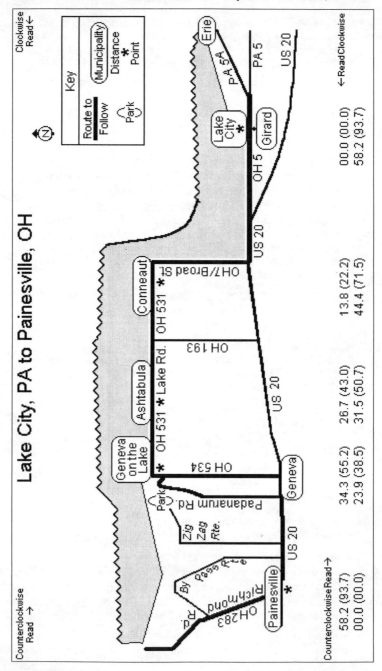

Lake City, PA to Painesville, OH

CRANKS

Look at your pedals as you spin them round and round. That crank is probably composed of three different pieces. Now remember way back when you rode that very first bicycle, the child sized one. Ah! The freedom it afforded you! Ah! The good times racing 'round the block or down that hill, shouting back and forth with your friends. Ah! Nostalgia!

Most likely that wondrous transportation machine had a one-piece crank, an *astabula* crank! As you go through Ashtabula think back with fondness and delight. The crank wasn't developed or made here but most folks confuse the two words.

Flowing along these roads you'll encounter one of North America's first playgrounds of the rich and famous—the towns along Lake Erie's shore. Here presidents came to relax. Industrialists came to build mansions. You came to enjoy the sights of what was, is and will be.

Towards the end of this section your crank will meet the eastern suburbs of Cleveland. Relax. The Crankiness of the traffic will get you nowhere in a hurry.

Clockwise Read down ↓	**Lake City, PA to Painesville, OH**	Counterclockwise Read up ↓
0.0 (0.0)	N. Lake Rd. @ PA 5/West Lake Rd.	58.2 (93.7)
	Travel West on PA 5/West Lake Rd. LAKE CITY/GIRARD: Refer to the Dunkirk, NY to Lake City, PA segment for information.	
10.0 (16.1)	US 20 Jct. PA 5 Continue Travelling on US 20/PA 5.	48.2 (77.6)
11.8 (19.0)	Ohio State Line @ Rts. 20/5 Continue traveling on US 20.	46.4 (74.7)
13.8 (22.2)	OH 7/Broad St. @ Main St./OH 2 Turn North on to Rt. 7/Broad St.	44.4 (71.5)

CONNEAUT

Info: Conneaut Tourism, 235 Main St., Conneaut OH 44030, 440 593-2402. AC: 440. ZC: 44030;

Attractions: Railroad Mus., 363 Depot St., 599-7878; Wineries: Conneaut Cellars, 12005 Conneaut Lake Rd., 382-3999; Rolling Hills, 768 S. Parish Rd., 599-8833; Biscotti Family, 186 Park Ave., 593-6766; Markko Vineyard, 4500 S. Ridge Rd., 593-3197.

Lodging: B&Bs: Bennett's Homestead, 263 Daniels Ave., 593-2237; Campbell Braemar, 390 State Rd., 599-7362; Day Street Inn, 955 Day St., 593-1226; Buccia Vineyards, 518 Gore Rd., 593-5976. Camping: Evergreen Lake Pk., 703 Center Rd., 599-8802; Windy Hill Golf Course & Cpgrd., 594-5251.

14.9 (24.0)   OH 531/W. Lake Rd.   43.3 (69.7)
                     @ Broad St./OH 7
Turn West on to W. Lake Rd./OH 531.
NORTH KINGSVILLE: **Attraction:** Tarsitano Winery, 4871 Hatches Corner Ridge, 224-2444. **Lodging:** Camping: Village Green Cpgd. (city pk.), 224-0310.

26.7 (43.0)   E. 6th St.   31.5 (50.7)
                     Jct. W. Lake Rd./OH 531
The road's the same, it's name is different!
Continue travelling West on E. 6th St./OH 531. Bridge St. in Ashtabula is a steep decent and assent.

ASHTABULA

Info.: Ashtabula Area CofC, 4536 Main Ave., Ashtabula OH 44004, 440 998-6998. AC: 440. ZC: 44004.
Services: All. Bike shop.
Attractions: Blakeslee Log Cabin, 441 Seven Hills Rd., 993-7846; Great Lakes Marine Mus., 1071 Walnut Blvd., 964-6847; Hubbard House Underground Railroad Mus., 1603 Walnut Blvd., 964-8168.
Lodging: B&Bs: Gilded Swan, 5024 West Ave., 992-1566; Harbor Lights, 809 Lake Ave., 964-2441; Peggy's, 8721 Munson Hill, 964-1996. Camping: Ashtabula Recreational Unlimited (ARU), 1420 Great Lakes Ave., 992 9445; Brockway Northcoast., 347 W. 24th St., 998-6272; Hide A Way Lakes, 2034 South Ridge, 992-4431; Luoma' Surfer's Point, 5649 Lake Rd. W., 964-6521.

27.5 (44.3)   Bridge St. @ E. 6th St./OH 531   30.7 (49.4)
Continue travelling on OH 531/Bridge St.

28.0 (45.1)   Lake Ave. @ Bridge St./OH 531   30.2 (48.6)
Continue traveling on OH 531/Bridge St., it bears South.

34.3 (55.2)   Geneva on the Lake @ OH 531   23.9 (38.5)
Continue travelling on OH 531.
Campers may want to stay the night here in Geneva On The Lake rather than continue on to Painesville.

GENEVA ON THE LAKE

Info.: Geneva-On-The-Lake CVB, 5536 Lake Rd., Geneva on the Lake OH 44041, 440 466-8600. AC: 440. ZC: 44041.

Attractions: Traditional amuesment park and indoor games (skeeball, etc.); Jennie Munger Gregory Mus., 5685 Lake Rd., 466-7337; Old Firehouse Winery, 5499 Lake Rd., 466-9300.

Lodging: B&Bs: CharLma, 6739 Lake Rd., 466-3646; Eagle Cliff Inn, 5254 Lake Rd. E., 466-1110; Lakehouse Inn, 5653 Lake Rd. E., 466-8668. Camping: Ralph's Place Cpgd., 4905 Lake Rd., 466-8091; Indian Creek Camping Resort, 4710 Lake Rd. E., 466-8191.

36.6 (58.9)   OH 534 @ OH 531   21.6 (34.8)
Turn South on to OH 534.
Alternative route to Painesville, See: *Geneva On The Lake To Painesville Zig Zag Route.*

37.9 (61.0)   Lake Rd. West @ OH 534   20.9 (33.6)
Turn West on to Lake Rd. W & enter the Park area.

38.5 (62.0)   Padanarum Rd. @ Lake Rd. W.   20.3 (32.7)
Turn South on to Padanarum Rd.

41.6 (66.9)   US 20 @ Padanarum Rd.   17.2 (27.7)
Turn West on to US 20.

GENEVA

Info.: Geneva Area CofC, PO Box 84, 866 E. Main St., Geneva OH 44041; Geneva City, 44 N. Forest St., Geneva 44041 OH, 440 466-4675. AC: 440. ZC: 44041.

Services: All.

Attractions: Shandy Hall Mus., 6333 South Ridge W. (Rt. 84), 466-3680; Old Mill Winery, 409 S. Broadway, 466-5560; Virant Family Winery, 541 Atkins Rd., 466-6279; Ferrante Winery, 5585 St. Rt. 307, 466-8466; Harpersfield Vineyards, 6387 St. Rt. 307; 466-4739.

Lodging: B&Bs: Polly Harper Inn, 6308 S. River Rd., 466-6183; Grapevine at Duckhill, 6790 S. River Rd., 466-7300; Lane Guest House, 235 S. Broadway, 466-3692; Last Resort, 4373 Coldsprings Rd., 466-6500. Camping: AJ's Cottages, 4925 S. Spencer, 466-1596; Audubon Lakes Cpgd., 3935 N. Broadway, Rt. 534 N, 466-1293; Geneva St. Pk., 4499 Padanarum Rd., 466-8400; Kenisee's Grand River Cpgd., 4680 SR 307, 466-2320; R&R Cpgd., 466-2550.

43.2 (69.5)   Lake County Border @ US 20   15.6 (25.1)
    Continue travelling on US 20.

50.0 (80.5)   Antioch Rd.   8.2 (13.2)
                    @ US 20/North Ridge Rd.
    Continue   traveling   on   US   20/North   Ridge   Rd.
    Counterclockwise cyclists can turn North on to Antioch
    Rd. and then follow the Painesville to Geneva On The
    Lake Zig Zag Close to the Lake Route.

66.6 (91.1)   Mantle Rd.   1.6 (2.6)
                    @ US 20/North Ridge Rd.
    Street name change to Erie St. Continue travelling on
    US 20.

58.2 (93.7)   Richmond St. @ US 20/Erie St.   0.0 (0.0)

PAINESVILLE

Info.: Lake County CVB, 1610 Mentor Ave., Painesville
OH 44077, 440 354-2424.
Services: Painesville to Cleveland bus: Laketran, 440
354-6100.
Attractions: Indian Mus. of Lake Co., 319   W.
Washington St., Lake Erie Coll., 352-1911. County fair.
Lodging: B&Bs: Fitzgerald's Irish, 47 Mentor Ave., 639-
0845; Riders Inn, 792 Mentor Ave., 354-8200.

Clockwise	**Painesville, OH**	Counterclockwise
Read down ↓	**to Lake City, PA**	Read up ↑

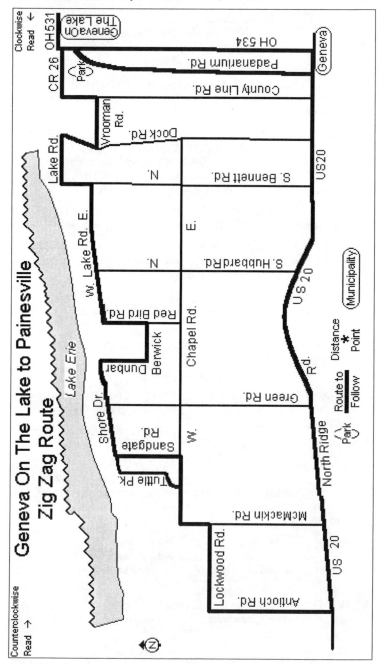

Geneva On The Lake to Painesville
Zig Zag Route

Clockwise	**Geneva On The Lake**	Counterclockwise
Read down ↓	**to Painesville**	Read up ↑
	Zig Zag Route	

Clockwise cyclist's Note: Although the distances using the Zig Zag route & the main route are about the same, the Zig Zag route will take a longer time to ride.

0.0 (0.0)   OH 531/Lake Rd.   11.1 (17.9)
                   @ OH 534/North Broadway
Turn South on to OH 534/North Broadway. OH 531 ends/begins at this point.   Counterclockwise cyclists turn East on to OH 531. Geneva on the Lake.

0.2 (0.3)   CR 26/Lake Rd. @ OH 534   10.9 (17.5)
Turn West on to CR 26. CR 26 is very easy to miss.

2.0 (3.2)   County Line Rd. @ CR 26   9.1 (14.6)
Turn South on to County Line Rd. Arcola Creek Natural Area will be almost in front of your wheel.

2.6 (4.2)   Vrooman Rd. @ County Line Rd.   8.5 (13.7)
Turn West on to Vrooman Rd.

2.9 (4.7)   Dock Rd. @ Vrooman Rd.   8.2 (13.2)
Turn North on Dock Rd. Turn South on Dock Rd. to go to US 20.

3.0 (4.8)   Lake Rd. E. @ Dock Rd.   8.1 (13.0)
Turn West on Lake Rd. E. The important point about this route is that Lake Erie is just North of where you are cycling.

4.1 (6.6)   Bennett Rd. N. @ Lake Rd. E.   7.0 (11.3)
Turn South on to Bennett Rd. N.

4.2 (6.8)   Lake Rd. W. @ Hubbard Rd. N.   6.9 (11.1)
Cross Hubbard Rd. N. and continue traveling on West Lake Rd. Traveling South on Hubbard Rd. will bring you to US 20.

5.0 (8.0)   Red Bird Rd. @ Lake Rd. W.   6.1 (9.8)
Turn South on to Red Bird Rd. You'll be traveling through a former "cottage" area now with year 'round homes.

5.2 (8.4)   Berwick Rd. @ Red Bird Rd.   5.9 (9.5)
Turn West on to Berwick Rd.

5.6 (9.0)   Dunbar Rd. @ Berwick Rd.   5.5 (8.9)
     Turn North on to Dunbar Rd.

5.8 (9.3)   Shore Rd. @ Dunbar Rd.   5.3 (8.5)
     Turn West on to Shore Rd.

6.5 (10.5)   Sandgate Rd./Tuttle Pk. Rd.   4.6 (7.4)
          @ Shore Rd.
     Turn South on to either Sandgate Rd. or Tuttle Pk. Rd.

6.9 (11.1)   Chapel Rd. W.   4.2 (6.8)
          @ Sandgate Rd./Tuttle Pk. Rd.
     Turn West on to Chapel Rd. W.

7.6 (12.2)   McMackin Rd. @ Chapel Rd. W.   3.5 (5.6)
     Turn South on to McMackin Rd.

8.2 (13.2)   Lockwood Rd. @ McMackin Rd.   2.9 (4.7)
     Turn West on to Lockwood Rd. Or continue traveling South
     to US 20.

9.6 (15.4)   Antioch Rd. @ Lockwood Rd.   1.5 (2.4)
     Turn South on to Antioch Rd.

11.1 (17.9)   US 20/North Ridge Rd.   0.0 (0.0)
          @ Antioch Rd.
     Turn West on to US 20/North Ridge Rd.

Counterclockwise note: Although the distances are
about the same the zig zag route will take a longer time
for you to ride.

Clockwise	**Painesville to**	Counterclockwise
	Geneva On The Lake	
Read down ↓	**Zig Zag Route**	Read up ↑

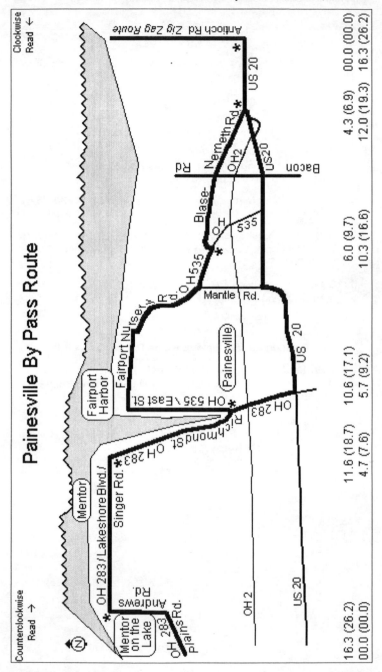

Painesville By Pass Route

Geneva On The Lake
Clockwise   **to Painesville**   Counterclockwise
Read down ↓   **Painesville By Pass Route**   Read up ↑

As you approach Painesville from the East you'll notice that US 20 suddenly has a sign forbidding bicycles on the roadway. In truth this sign applies to OH 2 rather than US 20. Ethically I can't tell you to disobey the law. Thus this nice Painesville By Pass Route.
The Painesville By Pass Route begins at the western end of the Zig Zag Route and can be considered an extension of the Zig Zag Route.
Visit Painesville for lodging or food.

0.0 (0.0)   Antioch Rd.   16.3 (26.2)
                   @ US 20/N. Ridge Rd.
     Turn West on to US 20/North Ridge Rd.

4.3 (6.9)   Blase-Nemeth Rd.   12.0 (19.3)
                   @ US 20/N. Ridge Rd.
Turn Northwest on to Blase-Nemeth Rd. The sign will say, "One Way." It's only a 1 way road for a ¼ mile to the solid waste facility. Thus watch for trucks for the ¼ mi. between US 20 & the solid waste facility. After the facility its clear sailing! Continuing West on US 20 will bring you directly into downtown Painesville.

5.3 (8.5)   Bacon Rd. @ Blase-Nemeth Rd.   11.0 (17.7)
Continue traveling West on Blase-Nemeth Rd. Counterclockwise riders/East bound cyclists can use Bacon Rd. to go to US 20 eastbound so that they do not have to cross busy US 20, there is a light at Bacon Rd. & US 20 but not at Blase-Nemeth Rd. & US 20. Turn South on to Bacon Rd., go under OH 2 and then turn East on to US 20.

6.0 (9.7)   OH 535/Fairport Nursery Rd.   10.3 (16.6)
                   @ Blase-Nemeth Rd.
Turn Northwest on to OH 535/FAirport Nursery Rd. This is a fairly narrow road with a few curves at the eastern end. Use caution. It isn't very heavily trafficked.

6.5 (10.5)   Mantle Rd.   9.8 (15.8)
                   @ OH 535/Fairport Nursery Rd.
Continue traveling West on Fairport Nursery Rd. Turn South on to Mantle Rd. to go into downtown Painesville.

9.1 (14.6)   East St./OH 535   7.2 (11.6)
                    @ Fairport Nursery Rd./OH 535
Turn South on to East St. Just follow the 535 signs! Turn
North on East St. to go to Fairport Harbor.

10.6 (17.1)   OH 283/Richmond Rd.   5.7 (9.2)
                    @ OH 535/East St.
Turn Northwest on to Richmond St./OH 283. OH 535
ends at this point. Going South on Richmond St./OH
283 brings you into downtown Painesville.

11.6 (18.7)   River St. @ Richmond Rd./OH 283   4.7 (7.6)
Continue traveling West on OH 283/Lakeshore Blvd./
Singer St.   Singer Ave./Lakeshore Blvd./OH 283 @
Richmond St./OH 283/River St. Turn West on to Singer
Ave. which becomes Lakeshore Blvd. Follow the OH
283 signs. Going North on River St. will lead you to
Headlands St. Pk. via Headlands Dr. GRAND RIVER
VILLAGE

13.2 (21.2)   Corduroy Rd.   3.1 (5.0)
                    @ Lakeshore Blvd./OH 283
Continue West on OH 283/Lakeshore Blvd. Cordury Rd.
leads to Sweet Nature Ctr. & Mentor Marsh ST. Nature
Preserve.

14.7 (23.7)   Buckeye Hiking Trail @ OH 283   1.6 (2.6)
Continue westward.
Trail head, undeveloped trail (2003).

16.3 (26.2)   Andrews Rd./OH 283   0.0 (0.0)
                    @ Lakeshore Blvd./Oh 283
Turn South on to Andrews St./OH 283.
MENTOR ON THE LAKE

Clockwise	**Painesville to**	Counterclockwise
	Geneva On The Lake	
Read down ↓	**Painesville By Pass Route**	Read up ↑

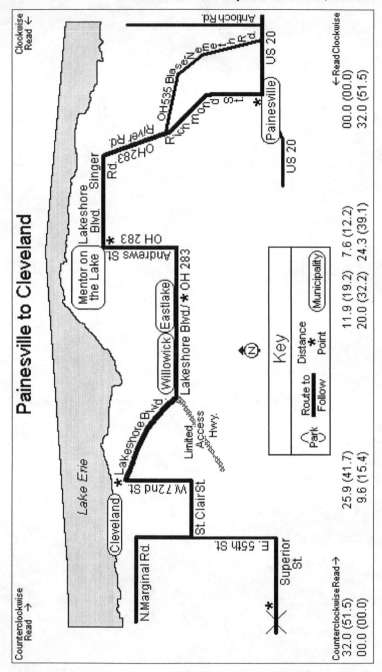

Painesville to Cleveland

HOMOGENEITY

If there is anything which really strikes me when I'm cyclotouring it is the homogeneity of North American cities. It does not matter from which direction you enter a city. It usually appears the same. A small industrial or office park followed by a series of suburbs alongside the four lane road lined with nationwide franchises and fewer locally developed businesses. A large retail shopping mall completes the picture.

For most residents and visitors it is neither a *pretty* nor an *ugly picture*. It is simply a fact of life.

This homogeneous view belies the differences among the people in each location. I'm not speaking of stereotypical ethnic differences but of individual differences that impart a different character to each location. Some of this *character* is due to the background of the 18th and 19th century original settlers. Some of it is due to later waves of immigrants from other nations and other places in North America. A significant amount of the character of an area appears to be attributable to the industry which dominates or did dominate the area. The geography plays a part too. Hills, mountains and chiseled valleys contribute to an expansive or contractive outlook of the area's residents.

Look beyond the surface. Seek out and talk with folks along the way. They really want you to tell them something. Anything! You are fulfilling their fantasy of the true meaning of liberty.

Clockwise Read down ↓	**Painesville to Cleveland**	Counterclockwise Read up ↑
0.0 (0.0)	Richmond St @ Erie St.	31.9 (51.3)
	Turn Northwest on to Richmond St. PAINESVILLE: Refer to the previous segment for information about Painesville.	
0.8 (1.3)	River Rd./Rt. 283 @ Richmond St.	31.1 (50.0)
	Bear Northwest on to River Rd.	
1.8 (2.9)	River Rd./Rt. 283 @ Singer Rd./Lakeshore Blvd.	30.1 (48.4)
	Turn West on to Singer Rd. Singer Rd. becomes Lakeshore Blvd. in about .25 mi. (.1 km.)	
6.7 (10.8)	Andrews St./Rt. 283 @ Lakeshore Blv./Rt. 283	25.2 (40.6)
	Turn South on to Andrews St.	

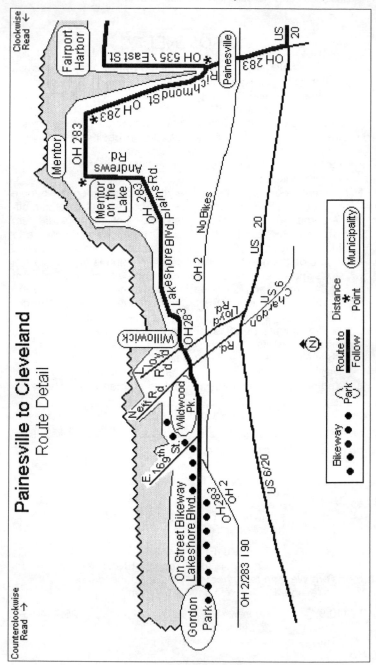

Painesville to Cleveland
Route Detail

7.6 (12.2)   Andrews St./Rt. 283   24.3 (39.1)
                    @ Lakeshore Blvd./283
          Turn West on to Lakeshore Blvd./Rt. 283

MENTOR ON THE LAKE
Info.: AC: 440. ZC: 44060.
Attractions: Holden Arboretum, 9500 Sperry Rd., 946-4400; James A. Garfield Nat'l. Hist. Site, 8095 Mentor Ave., 255-8722; Mentor Lagoons Nature Pres. & Marina, 8365 Harbor Dr., 205 3625; Headlands Beach St. Pk., 9601 Headlands Rd. (Rt. 44), 257-1331; Mentor Civic Ctr. Waterpark, 8600 Munson Rd., 974-5720; Mentor MarSh St. Nature Pres., 5185 Corduroy Rd., 257-0777.

11.9 (19.2)   Center Rd./Rt. 91   20.0 (32.2)
                    @ Lakeshore Blvd./Rt. 283
          Through travellers continue westbound
          Use Rt. 91, South to to to Cuyahoga National Rec.
          Area. EASTLAKE

14.6 (23.5)   Willowich City Hall   17.3 (27.8)
                    @ Lakeshore Blvd./Rt. 283
          Continue West on Rt. 283

15.7 (25.3)   Cuyahoga County Line   16.3 (26.2)
                    @ Lakeshore Blvd./Rt. 283
          Continue westbound.

19.6 (31.5)   Cleveland City Line   12.4 (20.0)
                    @ Lakeshore Blvd./Rt. 283
          EUCLID, suburb.of Cleveland.

22.4 (36.0)   Lakeland Freeway   9.6 (15.4)
                    @ Lakeshore Blvd.
          Continue West on Lakeshore Blvd. Landmarks: White City Park & Northwest Yacht ClubRt. 283 jct. with the Freeway. Lakeshore Blvd. becomes a 2 lane road.

25.9 (41.7)   W. 72nd St./Gordon Park   6.1 (9.8)
                    @ Lakeshore Blvd.
          Turn South on to 72nd St.

26.5 (42.6)   St. Clair St./Rt. 283   5.5 (8.9)
                    @ W. 72nd St./Rt. 283
          Turn West on to St Clair.

27.3 (43.9)   St. Clair/Rt. 283 @ E. 55th St.   4.7 (7.6)
          Turn North on to E. 55th St. Lakefront St. Park.

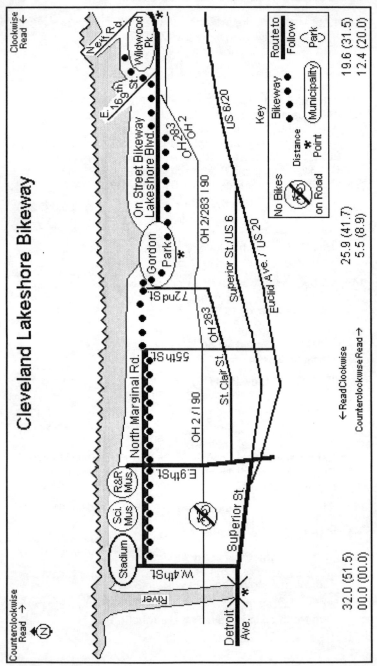

Cleveland Lakeshore Bikeway

27.3 (43.9)   North Marginal Rd. @ E. 55th St.   4.1 (6.6)
Turn West on to North Marginal Rd. Cleveland
Lakefront St. Park

30.7 (49.4)   Erie Side Ave. @ N. Marginal Rd.   1.3 (2.1)
Cleveland Stadium. Weave around the Stadium to
Front Ave.

CLEVELAND

Info.: Cleveland CVB, 50 Public Sq., Ste. 3100, Cleveland OH 44113, 216 621-4110. Cleveland Metroparks, 4101 Fulton Pkwy., Cleveland OH 44144, 216 351-6300. AC: 216. ZC: Various.
Services: All. Bike shops. Bike club:
Transportation: Amtrak, 200 Cleveland Memorial Shoreway N. E., 696-5115; Cleveland Hopkins Airport, 5300 Riverside Dr., 265-6030; Cleveland Transit bus, 200 Cleveland Mem. Shoreway NE, 696-5115; Greyhound, 1465 Chester Ave., 781-0520; Laketran (Painesville to Cleveland bus), 354-6100.
Attractions: Cleveland has all the attractions you can ever dream about.   Check the newspapers for street festivals and outdoor concerts. Museums: Children's Mus. of Cleveland, 10730 Euclid Ave., 791-7114; Cleveland Botanical Gardens, 11030 East Blvd., 721-1600; Cleveland Ctr. for Contemporary Art, 8501 Carnegie Ave., 421-8071; Cleveland Mus. of Art, 11150 East Blvd., 421-7350; Cleveland Mus. of Natural History, 1 Wade Oval Dr., University Cir., 231-4600; Great Lakes Science Center, 601 Erieside Ave., 694-2000; Rock & Roll Hall of Fame, 1 Key Plz., 781-7625; Steamship William G. Mather Museum, 1001 East 9th St. Pier, 574-6262; The Health Museum of Cleveland, 8911 Euclid Ave., 231-5010; Womens International Air & Space Museum, Burke Lakefront Airport, 1501 N. Marginal Rd., Rm. 165, 623-1111; African-American Mus., 1765 Crawford Rd., 791-1700; Cleveland Metroparks Zoo, 2900 Wildlife Way, 664-6500.
If you arrive in the middle of the summer, the music and theater offerings may be limited. Everyone likes a vacation!
Music: Cleveland Chamber Symphony, 687-9243; Cleveland Jazz Orchestra, PO Box 31666, 524-2263; Cleveland Lyric Opera, PO Box 93046, 685-5976; Cleveland Opera, 1422 Euclid Ave., Ste. 1052, 575-0903; Cleveland Orchestra, Severance Hall, 11001 Euclid Ave., 231-7300; Cleveland Pops Orchestra, 24000 Mercantile Rd. #10 765-7677.
Theater: Cleveland Playhouse, 8500 Euclid Ave., 795-7000; Cleveland Public Theatre, 6415 Detroit Ave., 631.2727; Cleveland Signstage Theatre, 8500 Euclid Ave., 229-2838; Dance Cleveland, 1148 Euclid Ave. Ste. 311, 861-2213; Great Lakes Theatre Festival, 1501 Euclid Ave. Ste. 423, 241.5490; Near West

Theatre, 3606 Bridge Ave., 651-2828;
The Flats: An entertainment district on the River.
Cleveland Pro Sports: Force soccer, Indians baseball,Barons hockey, Browns football, Cavaliers basketball, Rocker's women's basketball, Northfield Pk. race track, Thistledown race track,
Lodging: Motels and hotels downtown and in the suburbs. Many motels and hotels have specials. As in most major urban areas, there are no campgrounds and it is not a good idea to camp in the local parks.

31.5 (50.7)   Front Ave. @ Erie Side Ave.   0.5 (0.8)
     Turn on to Front Ave.

31.7 (51.0)   W. 10th St. @ Front Ave.   0.3 (0.5)
     Turn South on to 10th Ave.

32.0 (51.5)   W. 10th St.   0.0 (0.0)
                  @ Detroit Ave. Superior St. Bridge
     Turn on to Bridge walkway or roadway. This is a heavily trafficked bridge during rush hours and at various other times during the day.

Clockwise	**Cleveland to**	Counterclockwise
Read down	**Painesville**	Read up

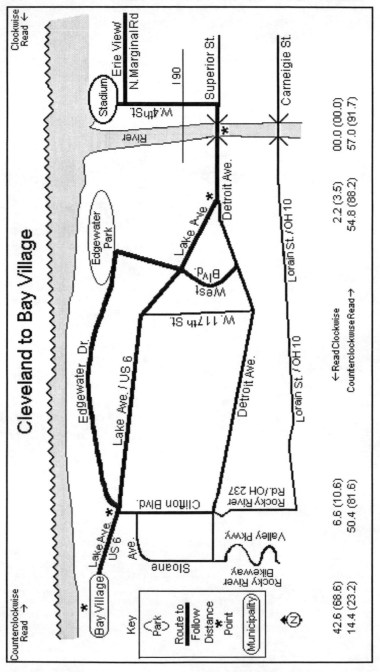

Cleveland to Bay Village

CENTRAL POINT

Cleveland is near the center of the southern half of Lake Erie. From Cleveland's docks goods could go southward deep into the mid-west by passing the Appalachian Mountains. At the same time the largess of the rich Ohio River farmland could be transported via the Lake and Erie Canal to Atlantic coast cities.

As Cleveland became an industrial center producing both capital goods and finished industrial products its importance grew. The waterfront and Cuyahoga River area became a major inland port.

Alas, points of time when a geographical location reaches its zenith of economic importance are fleeting at best. As industry moved to other areas of the United States and overseas so too did the environmental factors which made this area of the mid-west a not prized place to live and work.

Today all that has changed. The air and Lake are relatively clean. Residents and visitors flock to the shoreline to enjoy the trail along the water, the museums at the Lake's edge and the entertainment area along the River's edge.

The cities of Buffalo and now Detroit are emulating Cleveland's leadership in discovering the reasons why the Native Americans and first Euro-American settlers made this location so important. Those cities are slowly developing their Lakefronts into places delight.

Clockwise Read down ↓	**Cleveland to Sandusky**	Counterclockwise Read up ↑
0.0 (0.0)	Detroit Ave./Superior St. Bridge @ W. 10th St. Access Ramp/sidewalk. Enter ramp.	57.0 (91.7)
2.2 (3.5)	Lake Ave. @ Detroit Ave. Bear Northwest on to Lake Ave.	54.8 (88.2)
2.9 (4.7)	W. 104th St. @ Lake Ave. Turn North on to W. 104th St.	54.1 (87.1)
3.0 (4.8)	Edgewater Dr. @ W. 104th St. Turn West on to Edgewater Dr.	54.0 (86.9)
6.4 (10.3)	Webb Rd./Lake Rd. @ Edgewater Dr. Bear South on to Lake Rd.	50.6 (81.4)

6.6 (10.6)   W. Clifton Blvd. @ Lake Rd.   50.4 (81.1)
Through travellers Continue West on Lake Rd. Airport
arivees/departees join/leave here.

14.4 (23.2)   Lorain-Cuyahoga County Line   42.6 (68.6)
                     @ Lake Rd./US 6
Continue traveling on US 6/Lake Rd.
As you cross into Lorain County Lake Rd. changes its
name to Cleveland-Sandusky Rd.
An on road signed bikeway extends from the Lorain-
Cuyahoga County Line through Avon Lake & Sheffield
Lake Villages, about 5 mi. (8 km.). Watch out for the
sewer grates along the bikeway.
As you travel through Lorain County US 6 takes on
several names. Just follow the US 6 signs and keep
Lake Erie on your right side traveling West (on your left
side traveling East). BAY VILLAGE
AVON LAKE: **Attractions:** John Christ Winery, 32421
Walker Rd., 440 933-9672; Klingshirn Winery, 33050
Webber Rd., 440 933-6666.

25.6 (41.2)   OH 57 @ US 6   31.4 (50.5)
Continue traveling on US 6. West of Lorain US 6 has a
wide shoulder.

LORAIN
Info.: Lorain County CVB, 611 Broadway, Lorain OH
44052, 440 245-5282.
Lorain County Transit, 6100 S. Broadway, 949-2525.
Attraction: Moore House Mus., 309 W. 5th St., 245-2563.
Lodging: Motels.

34.9 (56.2)   Lorain-Erie County Border   22.1 (35.6)
                     @ US 6
Continue traveling on US 6. US 6 assumes several
street names as you travel East. Follow the US 6 signs.
Vermilion exists in both Lorain and Erie Counties so
don't be too confused.

35.9 (57.8)   OH 60 @ Lakeshore Blvd./US 6   21.1 (34.0)
Continue traveling on US 6/Cleveland-Sandusky Rd.

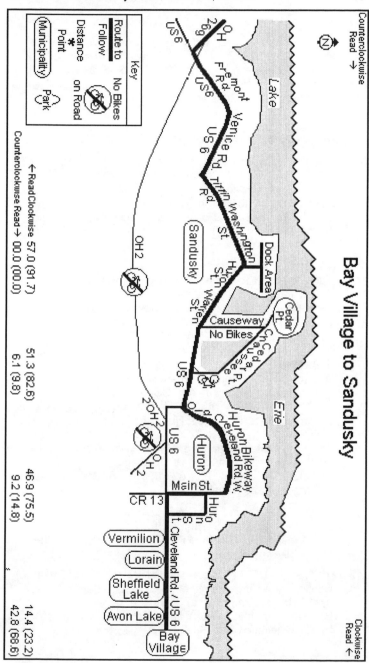

Bay Village to Sandusky

Counterclockwise Read →

Clockwise Read ←

Key

Route to
Follow
Distance *
Point
(Municipality)

No Bikes

on Road

Park

← Read Clockwise 57.0 (91.7)
Counterclockwise Read → 00.0 (00.0)

51.3 (82.6)
6.1 (9.8)

46.9 (75.5)
9.2 (14.8)

14.4 (23.2)
42.8 (68.6)

VERMILION
Info.: Vermilion CofC, 5495 Liberty Ave., Vermilion OH 44089, 440 967-4477; Lorain County Metro Parks, 12882 Diagonal Rd., LaGrange OH 44050, 458-5121. AC: 440. ZC: 44089.

Attraction: Inland Seas Maritime Mus., 480 Main St., 967-3467.

Lodging: Motels. Crystal Springs Cpgd., 31478 Bagley Rd., N. Ridgeville, 440 748-3200.

46.1 (74.2)   Huron St.   10.9 (17.5)
          @ US 6/Cleveland-Sandusky Rd.-
          Divided hwy.
Turn North on to Huron St. or turn North at the next traffic light, Main St. Follow Huron St. or Main St. into Huron Village. You will be following the on street Huron Bikeway signs.

46.9 (75.5)   Main St. @ US 6   9.2 (14.8)
Turn North on to Main St. and go into Huron Village. Follow the Huron Bikeway signs through the Village to Old Cleveland Rd. W. The Bikeway will bring you back to US 6 West of the "No Bicycles" section of US 6.

HURON
Info.: Huron CofC, 507 S. Main St.,; Huron OH 44839, 419 433-5700. AC: 419. ZC: 44839.

Attraction: Huron Municipal Boat Basin & Amphitheater, Main St. (off US 6), 433-5000; Huron Playhouse, Ohio St., 433-4744; Erie MetroParks, 3910 E. Perkins Ave., 625-7783; Huron River Greenway, Erie MetroParks.

Lodging: Motels. Camping: Huron River Valley Cpgd., 9019 River Rd., 443-4118; Cottage House, 5501 Cleveland Rd./Rt. 6, 627-8552; B&B: Captain Montague's, 229 Center St., 433-4756;

47.5 (76.4)   Cleveland Rd. W.   8.6 (13.8)
          @ Main St./Huron St.
Turn West on to Cleveland Rd. W. You are following the Huron Bikeway signs.

49.5 (79.7)   US 6 @ Cleveland Rd. W.   6.6 (10.6)
Continue traveling straight on to US 6. Counterclockwise cyclists travel straight on to Cleveland Rd. W./Huron Bikeway. Ride into Huron Village. You are avoiding a "no bicycles" section of US 6/US 2.

50.5 (81.3)   Shelton's Folly Nature Pres.   6.9 (11.1)
                  @ Rt. 6
No camping.

51.3 (82.6)   Cedar Pt. Rd./Cedar Pt. Chaussee 6.1 (9.8)
                  @ US 6
Continue traveling on US 6.
This road, Cedar Pt. Rd./Cedar Pt. Chaussee, is the only way for bicyclists to ride directly into Cedar Point Amusement Park.
You will not be permitted to bicycle on the toll road, *Cedar Point Causeway*, to the Park.
The road sign denoting this road, Cedar Pt. Rd./Cedar Pt. Chaussee, is usually covered with boards during the tourist season. You can identify this intersection by its Y configuration and the cement base of the covered road sign.
This is a very narrow 2 lane road along a spit of land. It is 5.5 mi. (8.8 km.) to the Amusement Park's parking lot toll booth and an additional mile (1.6 km.) to the attractions. Allow at least 1 hour to traverse this road to Cedar Point Park from US 6. No tent camping is allowed in the Park. There are motels/hotels at the Amusement Park. See Sandusky for very nice campgrounds along US 6 traveling West.

56.8 (91.4)   Jackson St.   0.2 (0.3)
                  @ Washington St./Huron St./US 6
Turn North on to Jackson St. to go to the ferry docks.

57.0 (91.7)   Sandusky Waterfront & Docks   0.0 (0.0)
                          SANDUSKY
Info.: Erie County/Sandusky CVB, 4424 Milan Rd., Sandusky 44870 OH, 419 625-2984. AC: 419. ZC: Various.
Services: Transportation: Amtrak; Greyhound, 6513 Milan Rd., 800 231-2222.
Ferry: Island Rocket (Cedar Pt., Kelleys Is. & Put-In-Bay), Jackson St. Docks, 627-1500; Goodtime I, Jackson St. Docks, 798-9763; Pelee Is. Transportation (USA-Canada ferry. Ferry to Canada may not sail every day), Jackson St. Docks, 800 661-2220.
Attractions: Eleutheros Cooke House, 1415 Columbus Ave., 499-2135; Follett House Mus., 404 Wayne St., 627-9608; Simpson-Flint House, 234 E. Washington St., 621-8679; Maritime Mus. of Sandusky, 125 Meigs St., 624-0274; Merry Go Round Mus., Jackson & W. Washington

Sts., 626-6111; Sandusky State Theatre, 107 Columbus Ave., 626-1950. Cedar Point Amusement Pk., PO Box 5006, 627-2350. Firelands Winery, 917 Bardshar Rd., 625-5474.

Lodging: Motels. B&Bs: Cottage Rose, 210 W. Adams St., 625-1285; Red Gables, 421 Wayne St., 625-1189; Wagner's 1844 Inn, 230 E. Washington St., 626-1726. Camping: Bayshore Estates Cpgd. (4 mi. from Cedar Pt. Rd.), 2311 Cleveland Rd. (US 6), 625-7906; Crystal Rock Cpgd., 710 Crystal Rock Rd., 684-7177; Martin's Marina, 4707 Martin Dr. (off US 6), 625-4703; Traveland Camp Sandusky, 3518 Tiffin Ave., 800 752-0186.

Clockwise	**Sandusky**	Counterclockwise
Read down ↓	**to Cleveland**	Read up ↑

Lake Erie Ferry Chart

Ferry	Mainland City	Island			
		Kelleys Is.	Middle Bass Is.	South Bass Is.	Pelee Is.
Jet Express	Port Clinton[1]			X	X
Miller Boat Line	Catawba		X	X	
Kelleys Is. Ferry	Marblehead	X			
Island Rocket	Port Clinton / Cedar Point	X		X	
Goodtime Cruises	Sandusky	X		X	
Sonny S	Inter-island only		X	X	
Pelee Flyer	Kingsville				X
Pelee Island Transportation	Leamington / Kingsville Sandusky[1]				X

[1] MV Pelee Islander provides daily international service; June-July, from Leamington; Aug.-Sept., from Kingsville. Jet Express has a limited cross the Lake schedule.

LAKE ERIE ISLANDS

The Islands! The Islands! You can go to the Lake Erie Islands by airplane, ferry and private boat. Ferry is the more romantic and practical way to cross the water.

Of the major Islands in Lake Erie Pelee Island is a Canadian National Park and International Biosphere site. Birders are almost as numerous as birds during the migration seasons in spring and autumn. It is best to access Pelee Island from Canada.

There are two cross-Lake Erie ferries between Sandusky and Leamington/Kingsville Ontario. The American ferry only operates one evening a week. The Canadian ferry operates every day.

The international ferries tend to have irregular schedules. Make certain the ferry is operating on the day you want to travel. Telephone the ferry two days in advance, the day before and the day you are planning to traverse the Lake.

There are three major Ohio Lake Erie Islands: Middle Bass Island, South Bass Island, and Kelleys Island. South Bass Island is also referred to as Put-in-Bay, its largest village. Each Island has its own character. Together they make a wonderful change for a day or two of cycling. The Islands provide a different perspective of the Lake.

Entertainment, groceries, restaurants, and lodging are limited on the Islands. Make certain that you bring sufficient supplies (food, beverages and fuel) for your sojourn.

There are opportunities to *island hop,* that is spend a half a day on one island then go to another island and finally go to a third island the next day. If you are planning to cross the Lake here then *island hop.*

The ferries depart from different villages on the mainland: Port Clinton, Marblehead, Catawba, and Sandusky. Consult the chart and confirm its information by telephoning the ferry company. Schedules, destinations and ability to transport bicycles have been known to suddenly change.

GENERAL ISLAND INFORMATION

Bicycling Info.: Bicycle route maps are available on each island. Bike rentals are available on all the major islands.
Services: Ferry service.
Goodtime Island Cruises, PO Box 2572, Sandusky, OH 44870, 800 446-3140/419 625-9692; Island Rocket/Island Express Boatlines, 101 W. Shoreline Dr., Sandusky OH 44870, 800 854-8121; Jet Express, PO Box 69, Put in

Bay, OH 43456, 800 245-1538; Kelleys Island Ferry Boat Lines, Marblehead Ferry Dock, 510 W. Main St., Marblehead, OH 43440, 419 798-9763; Miller Boat Line, PO Box 239, Put in Bay, OH 43456, 800 500-2421/ 419-285-2421; Pelee Flyer, 85 Park, Kingsville ON, 519 733-4611. Pelee Island Transportation, Pelee Is. ON N0R 1M0, 800 661-2220/519 724-2115.

KELLEYS ISLAND
Info.: Kelleys Island CofC, PO Box 783, Kelleys Is. OH 43438, 419 7462360. ZC: 43438. AC: 419.
Services: Restaurants, small grocery, bike rental.
Lodging: Motels. B&Bs: A Water's Edge, 827 E. Lakeshore Dr., 746-2455; Campbell Cottage, 932 W. Lakeshore Dr., 746-2740; Cricket Lodge, PO Box 323, 746-2263; Eagle's Nest, 216 Cameron Rd., 746-2708; East Shore Inn, 220 Lincoln Rd., 746-2130; Himmelblau House, 337 Shannon Way, 746-2200; House on Huntington Lane, 117 Huntington Ln., 746-2765; Inn on Kelleys Is., 317 E. Lakeshore Dr., 746-2258; Lakeshore Landing, 229 E. Lakeshore Dr., 746-2210; Morning Glory Inn, 134 Morning Glory Ln., 746-2560; Pascoe House, 111 Chappel St., 746-2705; Stoney Ridge, 120 Airline Rd., 746-2897.
Camping: Kelleys Island State Park, 920 Division St., 746-2546.
Attractions: The Island; State Nature Preserves; glacial grooves; and fishing.

MIDDLE BASS ISLAND
Info.: Middle Bass Information, PO Box 69, Middle Bass, OH 43446, 419 285-6121. ZC: 43446. AC: 419.
Services: Small grocery, restaurants, bike rental.
Lodging: Cottage & condo rentals. B&B: Middle Bass Is. Inn, 285-3802. Camping: St. Hazards Resort on the Beach, 1223 Fox Rd., 285-6121. Middle Bass Cpgd., 285-4403.
Attractions: Fishing, microbrewery.

SOUTH BASS ISLAND / PUT IN BAY

Info.: Put in Bay CofC, PO Box 250, Put in Bay, OH 43456, 419 285-2832. ZC: 43456. AC: 419.

Services: Small grocery, restaurants, bike rental.

Lodging: Hotels, motels & cottages. B&Bs: The Niagara Guest House, 681 Langram (Airport) Rd., 285-7447; The Stagger Inn, 182 Concord, 285-2521; Wisteria Inn, 1331 Langram Rd., 285-2828; Ashley's Island House, 557 Catawba Ave., 285-2844; Bay House Manor, 1360 Catawba Ave., 285-2822; Buck & Ollie's, 425 Loraine Ave. 285-2529; Byrnes' Trenton Guest House, 511 Trenton Ave., 285-2306; Ferrell House, 1940 LaPlante Ln., 285-4901; Getaway Inn, 210 Concord Ave., 285-9012; The Black Squirrel, 85 Cessna Dr., 285-7181; The Grape Leaf Inn, 215 Vintner's Cove, 285-2330; The Longhouse, 1589 Put-in-Bay Rd., 285-5664.

Camping: South Bass Is. St. Pk., 4049 E. Moores Dock Rd., 285-2112 (no reservations taken arrive early in the week for holiday weekends); Fox's Den Cpgd., 140 Conlon Rd., 285-5001.

Attractions: Perry's Victory & International Peace Memorial, National Park Service; Lake Erie Islands Historical Society: 441 Catawba Ave, 285-2804; Perry's Cave & Gemstone Mining, 979 Catawba Ave.,, 285-2405; Heineman Winery & Crystal Cave, 978 Catawba Ave., 285-2811; Stonehenge Estate, 808 Langram Rd., 285-6134; kayak rentals; parasail rentals; fishing.

PELEE ISLAND

Info.: See Leamington ON, for the complete listing.

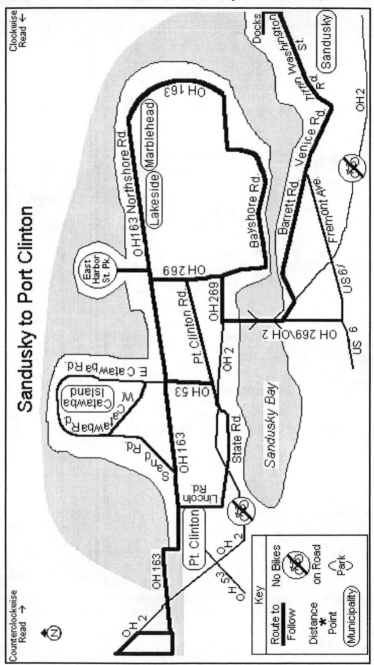

Sandusky to Port Clinton

ALONG THE SHORE

Traveling through Lorain on my way to Sandusky I stopped at the Park by the Lake. I drank in the beauty of the blue water, the clear sky and the joy of the people on the grass and in the water. It was one of those magnificent warm sunny days.

There, by the edge of the Park, were a group of teenage boys playing soccer. Not a particularly strange activity in 21st century America. The boys' shoeless feet were unique, for I had rarely seen it in other areas of this Nation.

When I was a 20 something and residing in Kenya, almost all the rural *football* (soccer) players, like almost everyone else in the village, were shoeless. The thick callus on their soles prevented minor abrasions from becoming major infected sores. True, they had to take utmost care to watch where they were walking but that callus was important to keep firm and solid.

Shoes, worn consistently by residents of developing nations are considered as both a status symbol and as a protection for the feet. A status symbol which sometimes had tragic consequences. When a person began to wear shoes, the callus became soft. It soon lost its protective power. If the plastic or leather clad foot's owner could not afford another pair of shoes or sandals the chances of injury to those precious soles were greatly enhanced if the callus did not return to its past hardness. In tropical nations, completely enclosed toe areas encouraged fungal growth due to moisture from sweat or when the shoe uppers became wet.

As in most clothing decisions, function must precede form rather than form preceding function.

It is good for those Lorain boys to develop their calluses. As they play they should imagine all their age group cohorts who lack shoes they take for granted regardless of the manufacturer's brand they must have on their feet.

Clockwise		Counterclockwise
Read down ↓	**Sandusky to Port Clinton**	Read up ↑
	Through Route to Port Clinton	

Fair Warning

It is difficult for bicyclists to cross the Detroit River, under their own power or via public transit, at Detroit MI/Windsor ON. You can neither ride over the Ambassador Bridge nor bicycle through the Windsor-Detroit Tunnel. The buses which traverse these crossings neither have bike racks nor allow bikes to be carried on them. There is a Michigan Department of Transportation pick up truck on call at the Bridge. The most efficient way of crossing the Detroit River at this point is to hitch a ride with a friendly pick up truck or van driver. A ferry is at Algonac ~50 mi./80 km. North of Detroit or 70 mi./112 km. North of Windsor (the distance discrepancy is due to Lake St. Clair).

Personally I like ferries. There is a ferry connecting Sandusky OH with Leamington/Kingsville ON. Using this ferry will reduce your distance by about 150 mi./ 240 km. I'll never tell anyone that you did not go all the way to Detroit/Windsor and thus did not *truly do the Lake*!

Note

Cyclists traveling to Toledo have several options. To go directly from Sandusky to Toledo; to stop and stay in either Port Clinton or on the Marblehead Peninsula or to go across Lake Erie by ferry from Sandusky to Leamington/Kingsville.

This segment, Sandusky to Port Clinton, is broken into its constituent parts:

Through Route to Port Clinton
Through Route Port Clinton to Toledo
Eastern Peninsula Route to Port Clinton via Marblehead.

0.0 (0.0)	Sandusky Dock @ Jackson St.	17.6 (28.3)
	Turn South on to Jackson St.	
0.2 (0.3)	US 6/Washington St.	17.4 (28.0)
	@ Jackson St.	
	Turn West on to US 6/Washington St.	
1.5 (2.4)	Tiffin Ave../US 6	16.1 (25.9)
	@ US 6/Washington St.	
	Continue traveling on US 6.	

2.5 (4.0)   Venice Rd./US 6   15.1 (24.3)
                   @ Tiffin Ave./US 6
Turn West on to Venice Rd./US 6.
Follow the US 6 signs.

4.4 (7.1)   US 6/Fremont Rd.   13.2 (21.2)
                   @ Venice Rd./Barrett Rd.
Ride straight on Venice Rd. on to Barrett Rd. The sign
states, *To Bay View*. Do not follow US 6. It's actually
easier and safer entering OH 269/OH 2 closer to the
causeway than further south where US 6 intersects with
OH 269. You could continue traveling on US 6 to OH
269 and turn North on to OH 269/OH 2.

7.6 (12.2)   Martins Pt. Rd. @ Barrett Rd.   10.0 (16.1)
Turn South on to Martins Pt. Rd.

8.1 (13.0)   OH 2/OH 269 Access Ramp   9.5 (15.3)
                   @ Martins Pt. Rd.
Enter OH 2/OH 269 going North/West. Ride only on the
wide shoulder. Be very careful as you ride on the OH 2
causeway.

10.4 (16.7)   OH 269 Exit @ OH 2   7.2 (11.6)
Exit on to OH 269 ramp. OH 2 is a limited access
highway. You must exit on to OH 269.

10.9 (17.5)   OH 269 Exit Ramp @ OH 269   6.7 (10.8)
Turn North on to OH 269.

Note: You have several options at this intersection.
1. Continue traveling around Lake Erie; going directly to
Port Clinton using the *Through Route to Port Clinton &
Toledo*.
2. Tour the Marblehead Peninsula and then continue
traveling around the Lake using the *Marblehead
Peninsula Route* (which is after the Through Route to
Port Clinton & Toledo).
3. Take a ferry to the Lake Erie Islands from Port
Clinton or Marblehead and then a ferry to Pelee Island
ON or Leamington/Kingsville ON.

11.4 (18.3)   Port Clinton/Eastern Rd.   6.2 (10.0)
                   @ OH 269
Turn West on to Port Clinton Rd. Turning East on to
Eastern Rd. will eventually bring you to Marblehead.
Continuing due North on OH 269 will bring you to East
Harbor St. Pk. (camping).

13.0 (20.9)   OH 53   4.6 (7.4)
                    @ Port Clinton Rd./State Rd.
Continue traveling on Port Clinton Rd.   Pt. Clinton changes its name to State Rd. at this intersection. As you enter Port Clinton it changes its name to State St. Turn North on to OH 53 to go to Catawba Island.

16.9 (27.2)   Lincoln Dr. @ State St.   .7 (1.1)
Turn North, towards Lake Erie, on to Lincoln Dr.

17.1 (27.5)   Perry St./OH 163 @ Fulton St.   .5 (.8)
Turn West on to Perry St./OH 163.

17.6 (28.3)   Monroe St. @ OH 163/Perry St.   0.0 (0.0)
You will probably stop and spend the night in swinging Port Clinton. It is approximately 30 mi. (48 km.) to Toledo from Pt. Clinton. If you're traveling directly to Toledo then continue traveling West on OH 163/ Lakeshore Dr. Lakeshore Dr. can be very heavily trafficked during the tourist season.

PORT CLINTON

Info.: Ottawa County VB, 770 SE Catawba Rd., Port Clinton OH 43452; 419 734-4386; Port Clinton Area CofC, 304 Madison St., 419 734-5503, Port Clinton OH 43452. AC: 419. ZC: 43452.

Services: Ferry: Island Rocket, Docks, 627-1500; Kelleys Is. Ferry, 510 W. Main St., 798-9763;

Attractions: Pt. Clinton Lighthouse, Brad's Marina; Walking Tour of 31 historical sites, Contact Pt. Clinton CVB; Crane Creek St. Pk. & Magee Marsh Wildlife Area, Rt. 2, 17 mi. W. of Pt. Clinton, 898-0960; Mon Ami Winery, 3845 E. Wine Cellar Rd.; Ottawa Nat'l. Wildlife Refuge, 14000 W. Rt. 2, 898-0014, Oak Harbor.

Lodging: Please remember that *Port Clinton* is a general address. The actual location of the lodging may be any place on the peninsula. Call ahead for directions.

B&Bs: Bashful Mermaid, 503 E. 2nd St., 734-3400; Dragonfly, 1586 Lockwood Rd., 734-6370; Five Bells Inn, 2766 Sand Rd., 734-1555; Inn at Speiss Harbor, 4495 W. Darr-Hopfinger Rd., 734-9117; Lake House, 702 E. Perry St., 734-5447; Marshall Inn, 204 Monroe St., 734-2707; McKenna's Inn, 5714 Pittsburgh St., 797-6148; Our Guest Inn, 220 E Perry St., 734-7111; Sand Road Lakefront Lodging, 2203 Sand Rd. 732-3949; Scenic Rock Ledge Inn, 2772 Sand Rd., 734-3265; Sunnyside Tower, 3612 NW Catawba Rd., 797-9315.

Camping: Cedarlane, 2926 NE Catawba Rd. (Rt. 53N), 797-9907; Chet's Place, 898-1104; Erie Island Resort & Marina, 4495 W. Darr-Hopfinger Rd., 734-9117; Family Camping Ctr., 2318 E. Harbor Rd., 734-5580; Golden Eye Family, 1030 S. Helendale Dr., 734-6646; Paradise Acres, 898-6411; Portage View Cpgd., 635-4479; River Retreat, 3830 W. Harbor Rd., 635-2472; Shade Acres, 1810 W. Catawba Rd., 797-4681; Sleepy Hollow Cpgd., 2817 E. Harbor Rd., 732-2088; Tall Timbers, 340 S. Christy Chapel Rd., 732-3938; Walleyes RV Park, 5115 E. Bayshore Rd., 435-3702.

Clockwise	**Through Route**	Counterclockwise
Read down ↓	**Port Clinton to Sandusky**	Read up ↑

Clockwise Read down ↑	**Eastern Peninsula Route** **To Marblehead & Port Clinton**	Counterclockwise Read up ↑
0.0 (0.0)	Rt. 269 Exit Ramp @ Rt. 269	27.8 (44.7)

Turn South on to Rt. 269

0.1 (0.2)   Bayshore Rd. @ Rt. 269   27.2 (43.8)
Turn East on to Bayshore Rd.

6.0 (9.7)   Johnson Is. Causeway   21.8 (35.1)
                   @ Bayshore Rd.
Continue traveling on Bayshore Rd. or ride a round trip
of 3.5 mi. (5.7 km) on to Johnson Is.

8.2 (13.2)   Marblehead Lighthouse   19.6 (31.5)
                   @ Bayshore Rd./Rt. 163
Take a break and see the lighthouse. Rt. 163 begins/
ends here.

9.2 (14.8)   Frances Dock Rd. @ Rt. 163   18.6 (29.9)
Island Ferries area.

LAKESIDE

Info.: Peninsula CofC, 210 W. Main St., 419 798-9777,
Marblehead OH 43440. AC: 419. ZC: 43440.
Services: Miller Boat Line, POBox 239, Marblehead, 285-2421.
Attractions: Lakeside Community, 236 Walnut Ave., 798-4461.
Marblehead Lighthouse St. Pk., 110 Lighthouse Rd., 797-4530;
Confederate Cemetary, Rt. 163, Johnson's Island Confederate
Officers Prison Cemetary, Gaydos Rd. off Bayshore Rd.
Lodging: B&Bs: Idlewyld, 350 Walnut Ave., 798-4198; Lake View
Historic Inn, 162 Walnut Ave., 798-5845; Maxwell's Hospitality
House, 239 Walnut Ave., 798-4527; Rothenbuhler's Guest House,
310 Walnut Ave., 798-5656. Camping:Fort Firelands, 5650 E.
Harbor Rd., 734-1237; Kamp Kozy & Marina, 2450 Meter Rd.,
732-2421; Marina del Isle, 6801 E. Harbor Rd., 732-2587;
Peninsula R.V. Park, 6930 E. Harbor Rd., 734-4778; Plymouth
Shore on the Bay, 8010 Bayshore Rd., 734-3570; Surf Camp, 230
E. Main St., 798-4823; Covered Wagon Cpgd., 5665 St. Anthony
Rd., 856-3058; Ottawa Lake OH.

MARBLEHEAD

Lodging: B&Bs: Ivy House, 504 Ottawa, 798-4944; Main Street
Inn, 818 W. Main St., 798-4440; Old Stone House on the Lake,
133 Clemons St., 798-5922; Victorian Inn, 5622 E. Harbor Rd.,
734-5611. Camping: East Harbor St. Pk., 1169 N. Buck Rd., 734-
4424.

14.1 (22.7)   Rt. 269 @ Rt. 163   13.7 (22.0)
Continue West on Rt. 163 to Port Clinton & 'round the
Lake. Turn North to go to East Harbor St. Park. Turn
South to go to Rt. 2 and counterclockwise around Lake
Erie.

22.9 (36.9)   Rt. 53 @ Rt. 163   4.9 (7.9)
Continue West on Rt. 163 to Port Clinton and continue
clockwise 'round the Lake. Turn North on to Rt. 53 for a
25 mi. (40 km) side trip on Catawba Is. Returning to Rt.
163 via Sand Rd. You do not have to return via Rt. 53 if
you are continuing westbound. Where Sand Rd. jcts.
with Catawba Rd. bear Southwest on to Sand Rd. to
continue westward to Pt. Clinton. Go straight on West
Catawba Rd. for 1.4 mi. (2.2 km) to return to Rt. 53 and
then South on Rt. 53 for .5 mi. (.8 km) to Rt. 163.

25.6 (41.2)   Sand Rd. @ Rt. 163   2.2 (3.5)
From W. Catawba/Sand Rd. intersection

27.8 (44.7)   Monroe St. @ Rt. 163/Perry St.   0.0 (0.0)
Downtown Pt. Clinton

Clockwise   **Eastern Peninsula Route**   Counterclockwise
Read down ↓   **To Port Clinton & Marblehead**   Read up ↑

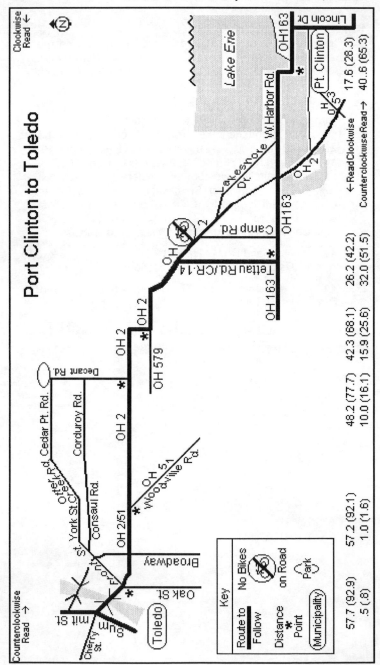

Port Clinton to Toledo

PLAYGROUND

Cycling along you'll see the beaches filled with folks enjoying themselves. I'm always amazed at how many folks are at the beach. Snowbirds who go to Miami Beach, Santa Barbara and Padre Island frolic in the summer on the Great Lakes.

Fresh water, entertainment, historic sites, and nearness to family and friends from long ago are significant attractions to bring people home again.

Enjoy the beach. Hop off your bike and jump into the Lake!

Clockwise Read down ↓	**Through Route** **Port Clinton To Toledo**	Counterclockwise Read up ↑
0.0 (0.0)	Lakeshore Dr./OH 163 @ OH 163/Monroe St./Perry St.	38.3 (61.6)

OH 163 bears Southwest and becomes Lakeshore Dr. after it crosses a barely noticeable bridge. Follow the Lakeshore Dr./OH 163 signs.

2.2 (3.5)	OH 163/3 Mile Crossing Rd. @ Lakeshore Dr./OH 163	36.1 (58.1)

Follow the OH 163 signs. This intersection is just opposite Ottawa Nat'l. Wildlife Refuge.

Lakeshore Dr. brings you to OH 2 which is a heavily trafficked limited access highway at this point. If you miss this intersection, don't worry, continue on Lakeshore Dr. to OH 2 and then turn Northwest on to OH 2. There will be a shoulder and the traffic will be fast moving. The most that will happen is that a police officer will stop you. With no other options and just a few miles of this divided highway the officer will let you continue on your way.

3.2 (5.1)	OH 2 @ OH 163	35.1 (56.5)

OH 2 is still a limited access highway at this point. Continue traveling on OH 163.

4.2 (6.7)	OH 358/Camp Rd. @ OH 163	34.1 (54.9)

Continue traveling on OH 163. OH 358 leads you to limited access highway OH 2.

6.3 (10.1)	Tettau Rd./CR 14 @ OH 163	32.0 (51.5)

Turn North on to Ottawa CR 14/Tettau Rd.

8.0 (12.9)	OH 2 @ CR 14/Tettau Rd.	30.3 (48.8)

Turn Northwest on to OH 2.

22.4 (36.0)   OH 579 @ OH 2   15.9 (25.6)
Continue traveling on OH 2.

23.7 (38.1)   Lucas-Ottawa County Line   14.6 (23.5)
                   @ OH 2
Continue traveling on OH 2

28.3 (45.5)   Decant Rd. @ OH 2   10.0 (16.1)
Through travelers continue on OH 2. Campers turn
North on to Decant Rd. to go to Maumee Bay St. Park
(camping). West bound cyclists do not have to double
back to OH 2 if they go to Maumee Bay St. Pk. Follow
the northern most set of roads on the Toledo map.

37.3 (60.0)   OH 51 Jct. OH 2   1.0 (1.6)
Continue traveling on OH 2/51.

37.8 (60.8)   OH 65 Jct. OH 2/51   0.5 (0.8)
Continue traveling on OH 2/51/65.

38.3 (61.6)   Summit St. Jct. OH 2/65   0.0 (0.0)
Turn North on to Summit St./OH 65.

TOLEDO
Info: Toledo CVB, 401 Jefferson Ave., Toledo OH 43604,
419 321-6404. AC: 419. ZC: various.
Complete Toledo information including a detailed map is
in the Toledo to River Rouge Section.

Clockwise	**Through Route**	Counterclockwise
Read down ↓	**Toledo to Port Clinton**	Read up ↑

Toledo, OH to River Rouge, MI

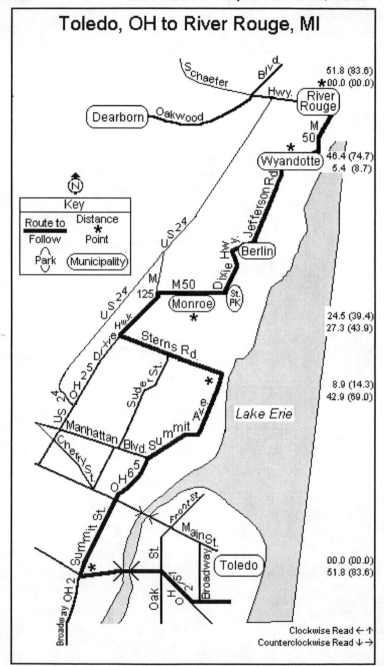

Clockwise Read ← ↑
Counterclockwise Read ↓ →

INDUSTRY

Some people say that Lake Erie ends at this point. As we learned in geometry class, an ellipse does not really have a beginning an and an end. What folks mean is that this is the western end of Lake Erie, just as Buffalo and Fort Erie are at the eastern end of the Lake.

Thanks to the geology of the rocks, climate, erosion and man (well, women too) geographical forms lack the symmetry of geometrical forms. Thus the Lake does not have perfectly rounded points and we will have to travel due north for about 50 miles (80 kilometers) along the Detroit River.

This is area is one of the prime manufacturing centers in the United States. You will be passing huge automobile plants as well as small factories supplying all types of goods to all classifications of industry. Some of what you see along side the road will dismay you. Many factories have closed or moved to other locations leaving behind rusting hulks of buildings. Others appear vibrant and to be belching pollutants into the air or water. In some cases the effluent being belched into the air is simply clear steam. In other instances those plumes of smoke are air borne contaminants possibly causing disease. The Great Lakes Commission monitors discharges into the Lake. Rather than viewing these industries negatively, think of the standard of living that American business and its workers have achieved for all the United States' citizens.

More importantly, as you bicycle this section reflect on the future of American manufacturing. What happens when there are fewer opportunities to be employed especially for those residents who are not academically achievement oriented? Now that the more highly educated residents of the United States are having their occupations go to lower labor cost producers in other nations what will happen to the economy.

The answer seems to be a growth of an oligarchy and tight linkage between large business enterprises and the political infrastructure which governs the Nation. Perhaps Dwight D. Eisenhower's warning about the military-industrial complex and its relationship to governance has become a truth rather than a supposition.

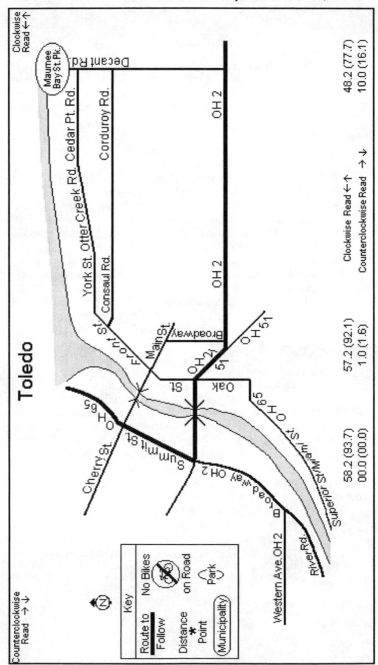

Clockwise	**Toledo** to	Counterclockwise
Read down ↓	**River Rouge**	Read up ↑

TOLEDO

Info: Toledo CVB, 401 Jefferson Ave., Toledo OH 43604, 419 321-6404. AC: 419. ZC: various.

Services: All. Toledo Area Bicyclists, 874-5839. Transit: Toledo Area Regional Transit Authority, 1127 W. Central Ave., 243-1241, bike racks on local buses. Amtrak Toledo, 246-0159. Shortbus Bus Lines, 476-3000.

Attractions: Arts Council of Lake Erie West, 1700 N. Reynolds Rd., 531-2046; Toledo Jazz Soc., Art Tatum Heritage Fest., 406 Adams St., 241-5299; Toledo Opera Summer Concerts, 255-7464; Toledo Symphony, Ballet, etc., 255-7464; Toledo (auto) Speedway, 5639 Benore Rd., 727-1100; Sandpiper Canal Boat, 2144 Fordway, 537-1212; Toledo Farmers Mkt., 525 Market St., 255-6765. Toledo Ctr. of Sci. & Industry, 1 Discovery Way, 244-2674; SS Boyer Mus. Ship, 26 Main St., 936-3070; Toledo Botanical Garden, 5403 Elmer Dr., 936-2986; Firefighters Mus., 918 Sylvania Ave., 478-3473; Toledo Mus. of Art, 2445 Monroe St., 255-8000; Toledo Zoo, 2700 Broadway, 385-5721. Parks: Metroparks Of The Toledo Area, 5100 W. Central Ave., 535-3050. Miami & Erie Canal Restoration, 5100 W. Central Ave., 535-3050.

Lodging: B&Bs: Cummings House, 1022 N. Superior St., 244-3219; Mill House, 24070 Front St., 832-6455. Camping: There are no campgrounds in Toledo. We are listing the towns along with the name/telephone number of the campgrounds. Toledo East/ Stony Ridge KOA, 24787 Luckey Rd., 837-6848, Perrysburg; Monroe KOA, US 23 at Summerfield, 856-4972, Peterburg; Big Sandy Toledo/Maumee KOA, 4035 SR 295, 826-8784, Swanton; Bluegrass Cpgd., 875-5110, Swanton; Covered Wagon Cpgd., 5639 St. Anthony Rd., 856-3058, Monroe MI.

0.0 (0.0)   Summit St. @ Rts.51/65/2   51.8 (83.4)
Turn North on to Summit St.
Summit is a very busy major street in downtown Toledo. Amtrak Station: Turn S on to Rt. 2. Travel 1 block to Williams St. Turn towards the River on to Williams St. The Station is at the end of Williams St. Toledo information is in the Port Clinton to Toledo segment.

0.5 (0.8)   Monroe St./51   54.3 (87.4)
          @ Summit St./Rt. 65
Continue North on Summit St. If the traffic is annoying you, turn towards the River on to Water St. then travel

North on Water St. The mileage is the same, only the traffic is different.

2.1 (3.4)   I 280 @ Summit St.   49.7 (80.0)
Continue North on Summit St. Summit becomes less trafficked and a 2 lane road.

4.4 (7.1)   Manhattan Blvd. @ Summit St.   47.4 (76.3)
Continue North on Summit St.
Alternative Route: Turn West on to Manhattan Blvd. for .5 mi. (.8 km.) At Suder Ave. turn North. Suder Ave. meets the main route at Sterns Rd. The mileage is the same.

7.4 (11.9)   Ohio-Michigan Border @ Summit St.
               44.4 (71.5)
Contiue North on Summit St.

8.9 (14.3)   Sterns Rd. @ Summit St.   42.9 (69.0)
Turn West on to Sterns Rd. This is an obscure turn just before the I 75 ramp. If you start to go up the ramp, turn around! and look for Sterns Rd. again.   If necessary, ask someone how to get to Rt. 125/Dixie Hwy.

11.0 (17.7)   Rt. 125/Dixie Hwy @ Sterns Rd.   40.8 (65.7)
Turn North on to Rt. 125/Dixie Hwy.

24.5 (39.4)   Rt. 50 @ Rt. 125/Dixie Hwy.   27.3 (43.9)
Follow Rt. 50 North through Monroe.

MONROE

Info.: Monroe County CVB, 106 W. Front St., Ste. C, 734 457-1030, Monroe MI 48161.

Attractions: Monroe Historical Soc., 126 S. Monroe St., 240-7780; M125 Monroe St. Scenic Byway, 120 E. First St, 384-9106; Lake Erie Metro Pk., 32481 W. Jefferson, 379-5020; Pte mouillee St. Game Area, N. Dixie Hwy.

Lodging: Motels. B&Bs.: Lotus, 324 Washington St., 384-9914. Camping: Camp Lord Willing, 1600 Stumpmier Rd., 243-2052; Harbortown RV Resort, 14931 Laplaisance Rd., 384-4700; Sterling St. Pk., 2800 St. Park Rd., 289-2715; Sunny South Villa, 15377 S. Telegraph Rd., 241-6466; Covered Wagon, 5665 St. Anthony Rd., 856-3058, Ottawa Lake; Monroe KOA, US 23 at Summerfield, 856-4972, Peterburg MI; Totem Pole Park, 16333 Lulu Rd., 279.2110, Petersburg.

27.8 (44.7)   St. Pk. Rd. @ Rt. 125/Dixie Hwy.   24.0 (38.6)
Continue North on Dixie Hwy.
Suggestion: If you are camping, this is the last
campground before Detroit, 35 mi (56 km) North. You
will arrive in Detroit at a more propitious time if you
camp here & continue North the next day.

33.5 (53.9)   Wayne-Monroe Cty Line   18.3 (29.5)
                  @ Dixie Hwy.
Continue North on Dixie Hwy.

39.0 (62.8)   Dixie Hwy. @ Jefferson Ave.   12.8 (20.6)
Dixie Hwy. changes its name to Jefferson Ave.
Lake Erie MetroPark (day use), 379-5020.

46.4 (74.7)   Bridge to Grosse Isle   5.4 (8.7)
                  @ Jefferson Ave.
Continue North on Jefferson Ave.   Jefferson Ave.
changes its name to Biddle Ave. in the Town of
Wyandotte. Take a side trip to Grosse Isle.

51.8 (83.4)   Coolidge Hwy @ Jefferson Ave.   0.0 (0.0)
Through travellers going to Detroit continue traveling
North on Jefferson Ave.
Turn West on to Coolidge Hwy. to go to Greenfield
Village/Dearborn.

DEARBORN

Info.: Metro Detroit CVB, 100 Renaissance Ctr., Ste.
1950, Detroit MI 48243, 313 259-4333. AC 313. ZC:
48124.
Attractions: Automobile Hall of Fame, 21400
Oakwood Blvd., 240-4000; Henry Ford Mus. &
Greenfield Village, 20900 Oakwood Blvd., 271-1620.
Lodging: Motels.

Clockwise	**River Rouge**	Counterclockwise
Read down ↓	**to Toledo**	Read up ↑

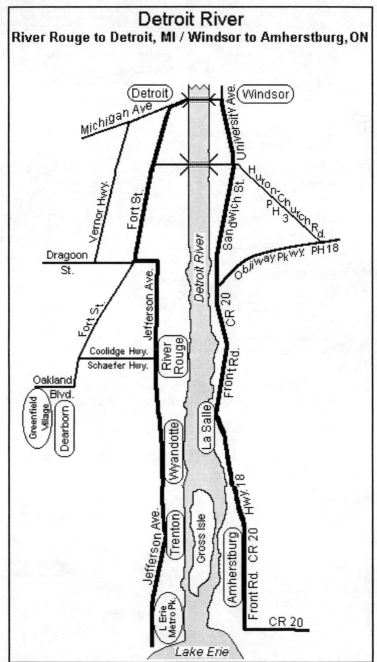

Detroit River
River Rouge to Detroit, MI / Windsor to Amherstburg, ON

COLLECTIONS OF HISTORY

Henry Ford really did change the world. For America, his use of an *assembly line* process for manufacturing a complex product at a reasonable cost was only eclipsed by his method of distributing and selling that product. The massive use of the motor vehicle as an efficient way to transport goods and people; to farm land and forest; and to provide the ultimate ability for individuals to escape the confines of their environment.

He must have known that this product would create an entirely different way of situating villages and conducting human interactions. The Henry Ford Museum and Greenfield Village in Dearborn might be considered his final testament to change. Preserve what was so that the next generation would be able to understand from whence they came.

Clockwise Read down ↓	**River Rouge to Detroit** **Direct Route to Bridge**	Counterclockwise Read up ↑
0.0 (0.0)	Coolidge Hwy. @ Jefferson Ave.	3.9 (6.3)
	Continue travelling North on Jefferson Ave.	
2.6 (4.2)	Dragoon St. @ Jefferson Ave.	1.3 (2.1)
	Turn West on to Dragoon St. Historic Fort Wayne.	
3.7 (6.0)	Vernor Hwy. @ Dragoon St.	0.2 (0.3)
	Turn North on to Vernor Hwy.	
3.9 (6.3)	Ambassador Bridge Entrance	0.0 (0.0)
	Enter Bridge Area. Hold up sign for a lift. Michigan DOT does have a pick up truck to transport bicyclists across the bridge. Theoretically there is a Windsor Transit bus with bike racks tjat goes through the Detroit-Windsor Tunnel. I have not been able to find any information about this bus. Apparantly the bike rack is too wide to permit 2 lanes of traffic in the Tunnel. Windsor Transit	

Clockwise Read down ↓	**River Rouge to Detroit** **Direct Route to Tunnel**	Counterclockwise Read up ↑

Clockwise Read down ↓	**River Rouge to Detroit** **Direct Route to Tunnel**	Counterclockwise Read up ↑
0.0 (0.0)	Coolidge Hwy. @ Jefferson St. Continue travelling North on Jefferson Ave.	6.9 (11.1)
2.6 (4.2)	Dragoon St. @ Jefferson Ave. Turn West on to Dragoon St.	4.3 (6.9)
3.4 (5.5)	Fort St. @ Dragoon St. Turn North on to Fort St.	3.5 (5.6)
6.7 (10.8)	Woodward @ Fort St. Turn East on to Woodward	0.2 (0.3)
6.8 (10.9)	Larned @ Woodward Turn North on to Larned St.	0.1 (0.2)
6.9 (11.1)	Beaubien @ Larned Turn East on to Beaubien Detroit Windsor Tunnel, 100 E. Jefferson, 313 (Detroit side) 567-4422; Detroit MI 48226.	0.0 (0.0)

Clockwise Read down ↓	**River Rouge to Detroit** **Direct Route to Tunnel**	Counterclockwise Read up ↑

| Clockwise | **River Rouge to Detroit** | Counterclockwise |
| Read down ↓ | **via Greenfield Village/Dearborn** | Read up ↑ |

0.0 (0.0)   Coolidge Hwy. @ Jefferson Ave.   6.1 (9.8)
     Turn West on to Coolidge Hwy.

0.5 (0.8)   Schafer Hwy. Jct Cooolidge Hwy.   5.6 (9.0)
     Continue West on Schafer Hwy

1.9 (3.1)   Oakwood Blvd. @ Schafer Hwy.   4.2 (6.8)
     Turn Southwest on to Oakwood Blvd.

6.1 (9.8)   Greenfield Village   0.0 (0.0)
                   @ Oakwood Blvd.
     Enter Museum area.

Clockwise Traveler Note: After visiting the museum you can
Directly to Detroit via Oakwood Blvd.! Simply travel East on
Oakwood (opposite direction from whence you came.

0.0 (0.0)   Greenfield Village   7.6 (12.2)
                   @ Oakwood Blvd.
     Turn East on to Oakwood Blvd.

6.1 (9.8)   Schafer Hwy. @ Oakwood Blvd.   3.4 (5.5)
     Continue travelling East/North on Oakwood Blvd.

7.2 (11.6)   Rouge River @ Oakwood Blvd.   2.3 (3.7)
     Continue travelling North on Oakwood. Oakwood changes it
     name to Fort St.

9.5 (15.3)   Livernois St. @ Fort St.   1.0 (1.6)
     Through travellers continue North on Fort St. Turn East
     if you want to visit Historic Fort Wayne

9.8 (15.7)   Dragoon St. @ Fort St.   0.8 (1.3)
     Turn West on to Dragoon St.

10.3 (16.6)   Vernor Hwy. @ Dragoon St.   0.2 (0.3)
     Turn North on to Vernor.

10.5 (16.9)   Ramp to Ambassador Bridge   0.0 (0.0)
                     @ Vernor Hwy
     Enter Bridge Area

| Clockwise | **Detroit to River Rouge** | Counterclockwise |
| Read down ↓ | **via Greenfield Village/Dearborn** | Read up ↑ |

DETROIT

Info.: Detroit Metro CVB, 211 W. Fort St., Detroit MI 48226, 202-1800. AC: 313. ZC: various. Greektown Merchants Assoc., 400 Monroe Ave., 963-3357.

Services: All. Transportation: Bicyclist's Suitability Maps, SE Michigan Council of Governments, 1900 Edison Pl., 961-4266; To cross either the Detroit River either by the bridge or the tunnel you must telephoe the Detroit DOT, 1301 E. Warren Ave., 933-1300; Ambassador Bridge, Lafayette & 21st St., 849-5244 Detroit Windsor Tunnel, 100 E. Jefferson, 567-4422. Public transit: Amtrak Detroit 11 W. Baltimore Ave (Mich. Ave & Greenfield), 873-3442; Detroit Greyhound Station, 1001 Howard St.

Attractions: Music, Drama, Museums: Detroit Opera, 1526 Broadway, 961-3500; Detroit Symphony, 3711 Woodward Ave., 576-5111; Gem Theatre, 333 Madison Ave., 963-9800; Hilberry Theater, 4743 Cass, 577-2972; Second City, 2301 Woodward Ave., 965-2222; Tiger Baseball, Coamerica Pk., 2100 Woodward Ave., 962-4000; Festivals; Anna Scripps Whitcomb Conservatory, Belle Isle, 852-4065; Charles H. Wright Mus. of Af. Am. Hist., 315 E. Warren Ave., 494-5800; Detroit Hist. Mus, 5401 Woodward Ave., 833-1805; Detroit Inst. of Arts, 5200 Woodward Ave., 833-7900; Detroit Science Center, 5020 John R. St., 577-8400; Fisher Mansion, 383 Lenox, 331-6740; Motown Hist. Mus., 2648 W. Grand Blvd., 875-2264; Mus. of African American Hist., 301 Frederick Douglass, 833-9800; Dossin Great Lakes Mus., 100 Strand Dr., 852-4051, Belle Isle.

Museums: Detroit Opera, 1526 Broadway, 961-3500; Detroit Symphony, 3711 Woodward Ave., 576-5111; Gem Theatre, 333 Madison Ave., 963-9800; Hilberry Theater, 4743 Cass, 577-2972; Second City, 2301 Woodward Ave., 965-2222; Tiger Baseball, Coamerica Pk., 2100 Woodward Ave., 962-4000; Festivals; Anna Scripps Whitcomb Conservatory, Belle Isle, 852-4065; Charles H. Wright Mus. of Af. Am. Hist., 315 E. Warren Ave., 494-5800; Detroit Hist. Mus, 5401 Woodward Ave., 833-1805; Detroit Inst. of Arts, 5200 Woodward Ave., 833-7900; Detroit Science Center, 5020 John R. St., 577-8400; Fisher Mansion, 383 Lenox, 331-6740; Motown Hist. Mus., 2648 W. Grand Blvd., 875-2264; Mus. of African American Hist., 301 Frederick Douglass, 833-9800; Belle Isle Pk., MacArthur Bridge, 267-7115; Dossin Great Lakes Mus., 100 Strand Dr., 852-4051, Belle Isle; Detroit Zoo, 8450 W. 10 Mile Rd., Royal Oak MI, 248 398-0900.

Lodging: Motels in the suburbs. Downtown hotels.

Detroit River
River Rouge to Detroit, MI / Windsor to Amherstburg, ON

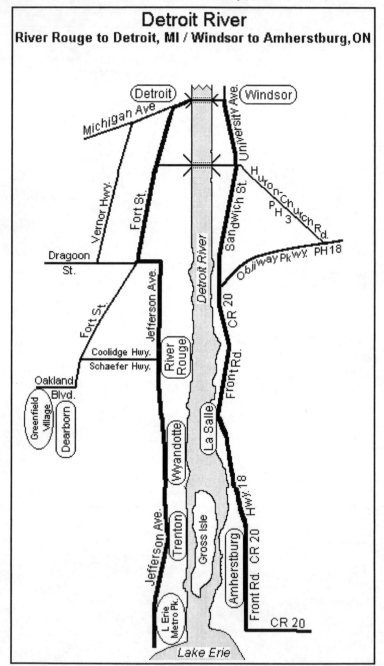

URBAN TO RURAL

I went to lunch today with a friend. Not a particularly strange occurrence for anyone who has a bit of disposable cash. It's a simple and usually enjoyable form of entertainment at a relatively low cost. You have the option of choosing your level of participation by the prices on the menu.

The luncheon spot wasn't one of those tablecloth types of restaurants. The tables were of Formica® the booths of naugahide. The counter was lined with stools which turned round and round on their chromium pedestals. Not one of those new fancy fast food places but an older diner type restaurant without the external appearance of a railroad *diner.*

Looking at the other patrons, creating scenarios about their lives based purely on external cues makes the time pass more quickly. Their physical appearance, clothing, body language, eating habits, what they are eating, and partially overheard speech patterns all contribute to the building of a character for these unknown folks. It matters little the true nature of the *character.* How the character fits the scenario in my mind is important. Many times the assumptions I made about the real person were incongruent with the person's real nature. That's fine.

This little vignette tells more about how to use some of those interminable moments as you bicycle long distances. Create, in your mind, scenarios. When you stop for a break, write in your notebook, the thoughts you have harbored as you cycled. It is better to write than to use a more modern mode of recording your thoughts. When you write something you are using more senses than when you are simply speaking into a recording devise. You are using the tactile sense of moving a pen across a sheet of paper. Your visual sense is being stimulated. Aurally you are hearing your sub-vocalization as it reverberates through the bones of your skull.

Bicycle touring is drinking in and recording in your mind all the cues which you encounter. Build your scenario for the joy of your memories and the memories of others.

Distances for Planning		
Distance between Towns	Towns	Cumulative Distance
31.5 (50.5)	Windsor to Malden	31.5 (50.5)
36.7 (59.1)	Malden to Leamington	68.2 (109.5)
9.7 (15.6)	Leamington to Wheatley Direct via hwy. 3	77.9 (125.4)
25.4 (40.9)	Leamington to Wheatley via Point Pelee National Park	93.6 (150.3)

Note

This segment, Windsor to Wheatley, is divided into four parts and provides
different options for touring. You make the decision!
Option 1: Travel directly to Wheatley
Option 2: Travel to Malden stay overnight, then continue cycling to Leam-
ington and visit Point Pelee National Park
Option 3: Travel directly to Leamington then go to Point Pelee National
Park and either return to Leamington or go to directly to
Wheatley.
Option 4: Travel from Leamington or Kingsville to Pelee Island ON or San-
dusky OH USA.

Clockwise	**Windsor to Malden**	Counterclockwise
Read down ↑	**Ambassador Bridge Route**	Read up ↑

0.0 (0.0)   Huron Church Rd.   2.0 (3.2)
                 @ University Ave.
        Turn South on to University Ave.

1.4 (2.3)   Prince St. @ University Ave.   0.6 (1.0)
        Turn West on to Prince St.

2.0 (3.2)   Sandwich St./Ojibway Pkwy.   0.0 (0.0)
                 @ Prince St.
        Turn South on to Sandwich St./Ojibway Pkwy. and
        follow the directions in the Windsor to Malden segment.

Clockwise	**Malden to Windsor**	Counterclockwise
Read down ↑	**Ambassador Bridge Route**	Read up ↑

Clockwise Read down ↓	**Windsor to Malden** **Tunnel Route**	Counterclockwise Read up ↑

0.0 (0.0)   Bus Terminal @ University Ave.   31.4 (50.5)
Turn South on to University Ave. W

WINDSOR

Info.: CVB of Windsor, Essex & Pelee Island, 333 Riverside Dr. W., Ste., 103, Windsor ON N9A 5K4, 519 255-6530. Ontario Travel Info Ctre, 1235 Huron Church Rd., 973-1310. AC 519. PC (Postal Code): various.

Services: Detroit Windsor Tunnel, Windsor Tunnel Commission, c/o Detroit Canada Tunnel Comm., Ouellette St., 258-7424; Ambassador Bridge (bicyclist's prohibited), 313 849-5244. Transit Windsor, 3700 North Service Rd. E., 944-4111; VIARail Canada, 298 Walker Rd., 256-5511;

Attractions: Ojibway Nature Ctr., 966-5852; Casino Windsor, & other bingo & casinos, Riverside Dr., 519 258-7878; Windsor Raceway, Hwy. 18, 969-8311; Windsor Symphony, 487 Ouellette Ave., 973-1238; Windsor Theatres, see local newspaper; Via Italia - Windsor's Little Italy, 573 Erie St. E., 974-2526; Art Gallery of Windsor, 401 Riverside Dr. W., 977-0013; François House, 254 Pitt St. W., 519 263-1812; Underground Railroad Mus., 932 Conc. 6, 258-6253; Windsor Wood Carving Mus., 850 Ouellette Ave., 977-0823; Canadian Hist. Aircraft Assoc., Windsor Airport, 966-9742; Ford City Discovery Ctr., 1012 Drouillard Rd., 254-4055; Mackenzie Hall, 3277 Sandwich St., 255-7600; Willistead Manor, 1899 Niagara St., 253-2365; Community Mus., 254 Pitt St. W., 253-1812; Coventry Gardens, Riverside Dr. E., 255-6276.

Lodging: Motels. B&Bs: Amber Sunset, 1575 Riverside Dr. W., 256-3031; Berry Patch, 1521 Wentworth, 250-0264; Branteaney's, 1649 Chappus St., 966-2334; Devonshire House, 546 Devonshire Rd., 256-8124; Diotte, 427 Elm Ave., 792-3072; Kirk's, 406 Moy Ave., 255-9346; River Park Terrace, 747 Chatham St. E., 252-3498; Univ. of Windsor Summer Accommodation, 401 Sunset Ave., May-Aug:973-7074 Sept-Apr 253-3000x3388; Welcome Home, 3857 Riverside Dr. E., 945-8255;
Ye Olde Walkerville, 1104 Monmouth Rd., 254-1507; Camping: KOA Windsor4855 Conc. 9, SS RR 3, 735-3660, Maidstone ON; The Windsor Campground, 4855 Conc. 9, S.S. R. R. 3, 735-3660.

3.1 (5.0)   Riverside Dr./Sandwich St.   28.3 (45.5)
@ University Ave.
Continue South on Riverside Dr./Sandwich St.

5.3 (8.5)   Prince St.   26.1 (42.0)
                   @ Sandwich St./Ojibway Pkwy./ PH 18
          Ambassador Bridge crossees join us here

7.6 (12.2)   E C Row Exway.   23.8 (38.3)
                   @ Ojibway Pkwy./PH 18
          Continue South on PH 18. The street name changes as
          you go though various townships. Follow PH 18 signs.

16.5 (26.6)   E 8 @ E 20/Front St.   14.9 (24.0)
          Continue South on E 20. E = Essex County road.
          LASALLE: **Lodging:** B&B: Nantais', 2240 Front Rd., 734-
          8916.

23.8 (38.3)   Simcoe St./E 18   7.6 (12.2)
                   @ E 20/Sandwich St.
          Continue South on E 18.

AMHERSTBURG

Info.: Amherstburg CofC, 116 Sandwich St. N., ; Amherstburg ON
N9V 2Z2, 519 736-2001. AC: 519.

Attractions: Project HMS Detroit & Gordon House, 268
Dalhousie St., 736-1133; N. Am., Black Hist. Mus., 277 King St.,
736-5432; Park House Mus. & Amherstburg Museums, 214
Dalhousie St., 736-2511; Fort Malden Nat'l Hist. Site, 100 Laird
Ave., 736-5416; Amherstburg Parks, 736-0012; D'Angelo Estate
Winery, 5141 Conc. 5, RR4, 736-7959.

Lodging: Motel. B&Bs: Patrician Inn, 1399 Front Rd. N., 736-
1549; Allen's, 259 George St., 736-6731; Be'v Blossoms, 54
Spring Ct., 736-5603; Bondy House, 199 Dalhouse St., 736-9433;
Honor's, 4441 Conc. 4 S, RR2, 736-7737; Patrician Inn, 1399
Front Rd. N., 736-1549. Camping: Holiday Beach Cons. Area, E
50, 736-3772; Yogi Bear Jellystone Pk., 4610 Essex Cty Rd. 18
RR 1, 736-3201.

29.9 (48.1)   E 50 @ E 20/Main St.   1.5 (2.4)
          Turn South on to E 50. MALDEN

31.4 (50.5)   Holiday Beach Consv. Area   0.0 (0.0)
                   @ E 50
          Stop here for the evening or continue eastward
          on E 50. Camping.

Clockwise	**Windsor**	Counterclockwise
Read down ↓	**to Malden**	Read up ↑
	Tunnel Route	

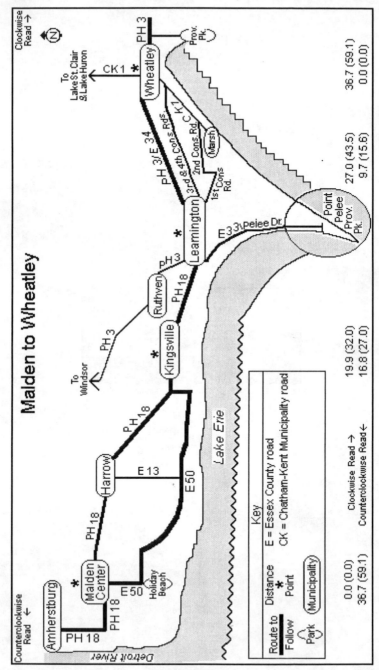

Malden to Wheatley

WATER CROSSING

Of all the animals which cross large expanses of water it is the
birds which are to be most admired. Yearly many bird species
travel thousands of miles twice a year.

Lake Erie is a major stopping point for migratory birds. The relatively shallow depth of the Lake provides excellent conditions
for the growth of algae, cattails, fish and other avian food
sources.

The Lake's latitude and large size creates weather conditions
which moderate the climate more than points further north.

Point Pelee and Pelee Island are the perfect Canadian National
Parks to spend a few days observing nature. They may appear to be like any other forested area but they are unique in
what the Pelee's have to offer birds and humans.

Malden / Holiday Beach to

Clockwise		Counterclockwise
Read down ↑	**Leamington / Wheatley**	Read up ↑

0.0 (0.0)   E 50 @ E 20   36.7 (59.1)

Turn Southeast on to E 50.
You can slightly shorten your trek by turning East on E
20 and take that road to Kingston. It goes inland rather
than along the Lake.
Amherstburg and Malden information is in the Windsor
to Malden segment.

1.5 (2.4)   Holiday Beach Consv. Area   35.2 (56.6)
                   @ E 50/Lakeshore Dr.

Continue East on E 50. Camping.
A bit further East is E 13. Turning North on E 13 will bring
you to Harrow. HARROW: **Lodging:** B&Bs: Mesman's
Manor on the Lake, 31 Levergood Ln., 736-6217; Twin
Maples, 631 Queen St., 738-3902. Camping: Epping Forest
Trailer Pk., E 50, 738-2811.

19.9 (32.0)   E 50/Lakeshore Dr.   16.8 (27.0)
                     @ E 29/Division St.

Continue East on E 20/Main St.

KINGSVILLE

Info.: Kingsville Business Improvement Assoc., 13 Main
St. W. Kingsville ON N9Y 1H2, 519 733-6250. AC: 519.
Services: Ferry to Pelee Is. & Sandusky, OH, USA: Pelee
Is. Transportation Co., Ferry Terminal, 724-2115/800 661-

2220.

Attractions: SW Ontario Heritage Village, 6155 Arner Townline, CR 23, 776-6909; Kingsville Hist. Pk., (Military Mus.), 164 Lansdowne, 733-2803; John R. Park Homestead Cons. Area, 915 CR 50 E.(@ Iler Rd.), 738-2029; Kingsville Parks, 733-2305; Colasanti Tropical Gardens, 3rd Concession Ruthven, 322-2301; Jack Miner Bird Sanctuary, 322 Rd. 3, N. (of Kingsville), 733-4034; Pelee Island Winery Store, 455 Seacliff Dr.733-6551.

Lodging: Motels. B&Bs: Dirks Cozy Comfort, 77 Division Rd. S., 733-5976; Edge of Thyme, 627 McCracken Rd., 733-6207; Hill N' Dale, 138 Division St. N., 733-5518; Kingswood Inn, 101 Mill St. W., 733-3248; Red Lion, 171 Division St. N., 733-3195; Vintage Goose, 31 Division St. S., 733-5070; Wedding House, 98 Main St. E., 733-3928; Camping: Pleasant Valley Cpgd., 808 CR 20 W., 733-5961.

27.0 (43.5)   Erie St./PH 77   9.7 (15.6)
                     @ E 20/Seacliff Dr./1st Cons Rd.

Turn North on Erie St./PH 77.

The Direct Route to Wheatley immediately follows the Leamington information. The Almost Direct Route to Wheatley is after the Direct Route.

Note: Pelee National Park is a day use only Park. It is a beautiful park with very fine trails, beautiful scenery, magnificent birds, and essentially without people.

Please remember that the **one way** distance from this intersection to Point Pelee in Point Pelee Nat'l. Pk. is 21 km. (13 mi.). Round trip distance from this intersection to Point Pelee is 42 km. or 26.2 mi. You must return to this intersection to continue eastward.

LEAMINGTON

Info.: Leamington Dist. CofC, 33 Princess St., 3rd Fl, Leamington ON N8H 3W3, 519 326-2721. AC: 519.

Services: Pelee Is. Transportation Co., Ferry Terminal, Leamington ON, 519 724-2115/800 661-2220.

Attractions: Hillman Marsh Cons. Area, E 37, 776-5209; Point Pelee Nat'l. Pk., 1118 Point Pelee Dr., 322-2365; Leamington Arts Ctr. & Erie Quest, 72 Talbot St. W., 326-2711; Grape Tree Estate Wines, 308 Rd. 3, 322-2081.

Lodging: Motels. B&Bs: Monica's, 765 PH 77, 326-6985; B&B with Ern & Anita, 1023 Rd. 2, RR 2, 326-4254; Bitter Suite, 11 Albert St., 322-5820; Do Drop In, 34 St. Joseph St., 326-5558; Erie Shores, 280 Robson Rd., RR 1, 326-2936; Home Suite Home, 115 Erie St. S., 326-7169;

Island View, 470 Talbot St. W., 326-0821; Leamington, 92 Oak St. E., 329-4378; Lotus Hall, 128 Bennie Ave., 326-2419; Marlborough House, 49 Marlborough St. W., 322-1395; Point Pelee B&B Res. Serv., 115 Erie St. S., 326-7169; Point Pelee B&B Serv., 216 Erie St. S., 825-8008. Camping: Sturgeon Woods Cpgd. & Marina, Pt. Pelee Rd., RR 1, 326-1156.

PELEE ISLAND

Info.: CVB of Windsor, Essex & Pelee Island, 333 Riverside Dr. W., Ste. 103, City Centre, Windsor ON N9A 5K4, 519 255-6530/800 265-3633.
Pelee Island: AC: 519. PC: N0R 1M0.
Services: Grocery, bakery, deli, and restaurants. No bank or atm on the island. Most businesses do take credit cards.
Ferry: Pelee Is. Transportation Co., Ferry Terminal, 800 661-2220/519 724-2115, from Leamington/Kingsville and Sandusky. If you are going to Sandusky OH, USA, call ahead. Make certain that you have the proper forms of identification. A passport is best. This ferry is an "international" ferry.
Bicycling Services: Comfortech Bicycle Rentals, West Dock, 724-2828. Bicycling maps: Pick up a free map. Bring extra repair kit and a tube. The roads are narrrow and may be gravel or loose chip seal. Use extreme care when bicycling on the Island.
Attractions: Pelee Is. Heritage Ctr., West Dock, 1073 W. Shore Rd., 724-2291; Pelee Paddler (kayaking rentals), 271A North Shore Rd., 724-2002; Pelee Island Winery, 20 East West Rd., 724-2469. Birding is the activity of choice on the island; Point Pelee Bird Migration Line, 322-2371.
Lodging: Motel. B&Bs: Nothing Fancy, 640 East West Rd., 724-9908; Sheridan House, 134 Sheridan Pt. Rd., 724-9947; Blueberry Hill, 85 N. Shore Rd., 724-1109; Gathering Place, 933 W. Shore Rd., 724-2656; Happy Haven's, 113 Sheridan Pt. Rd., 724-2918; Island Memories, 192 N. Shore Rd., 724-2667; It's Home, 1431 East Shore Rd., 724-2328; Stonehill, 911 West Shore Rd., 724-2193; Tin Goose, 1060 East West Rd., 724-2223; Twin Oaks, 751 East West Rd., 724-2434; Anchor and Wheel Inn, 11 W. Shore Rd., 724-2195. Camping: Anchor and Wheel Inn, 11 W. Shore Rd., 724-2195; East Pk. (Municipal) Cpgd., 1362 East Shore Dr., 724-2931; Dick's Marina, 256 S. Shore Rd., 724-2024.

	Leamington / Wheatley	
Clockwise		Counterclockwise
Read down ↑	**Malden / Holiday Beach**	Read up ↑

128   'Round Lake Erie: A Bicyclist's Tour Guide, 2nd. Ed.

Clockwise	**Leamington / Wheatley to**	Counterclockwise
Read down ↓	**Malden / Holiday Beach**	Read up ↑

Direct Route Wheatley to Leamington

27.0 (43.5)   Erie St./PH 77   9.7 (15.6)
                   @ E 20/Seacliff Dr./1st Cons Rd.
Turn North on Erie St./PH 77.

28.3 (45.5)   PH 3/E 34/Talbot St.   8.4 (13.5)
                   @ Erie St./PH 77
Turn East on to PH 3/CR 34/Talbot St.
PH 3 becomes a county road, E 3, here. The PH or Kings
Highway signs may still be on the road side.

36.2 (58.3)   CK 1 @ E 34/PH/E 3/Talbot Trail   0.6 (1.0)
Continue traveling East to go to Wheatley Prov. Pk.
Ontario is renumbering the road system. Provincial
Highway and the old King's Highway signs may still be
on the roads. *3* is the road number to follow!
You've crossed the county border and are now in the
Municipality of Chatham-Kent.

WHEATLEY
Lodging: B&Bs: Stonegate, 776 Hwy. 3, 825-3113; Erie
Buff, 2902 Talbot Trail E., 825-4472; Hillside, 282 Hillside
Ave., 825-4547; Royal Harbourview, RR 2, 825-7955;
Winter Wren, 21389 Zion Rd., RR 1, 825-7671; By The
Bay, 493 Gregory Line, RR 1, Box 1, Site 7, 825-7729;
Wild Rose, 21298 Harbour St., RR 1, 825-9070; Camping:
Camper's Cove, Campers Cove Rd., RR 1, 825-4732;
Holiday Harbour Resort, 20951 Pier Rd., 825-7396;
Lakeside Village, 2416 Talbot Trail, 825-4307; Wheatley
Prov. Pk., Klondike Rd., 825-4659.

36.7 (59.1)   Wheatley Prov. Pk. Rd.   0.0 (0.0)
                   @ CK/PH 3
Enter Park. This is the closest Park, east of Point Pelee
National Park and the Leamington/Kingsville Ferry which
permits camping.

Clockwise	**Leamington / Wheatley to**	Counterclockwise
Read down ↓	**Malden / Holiday Beach**	Read up ↑

Direct Route Wheatley to Leamington

Clockwise	**Leamington / Wheatley to**	Counterclockwise
Read down ↓	**Malden / Holiday Beach**	Read up ↑
	Almost Direct Route Wheatley to Leamington	

27.0 (43.5)   Erie St./PH 77   9.7 (15.6)
               @ E 20/Seacliff Dr./1st Cons. Rd.
Continue traveling East on
CR 20/Seacliff Dr./1st Cons. Rd.

31.6 (50.9)   Hillman Rd.   5.1 (8.2)
               @ E 20/1st Cons. Rd.
Turn North on to Hillman Rd.
Hillman Marsh Conservation Area.

32.5 (52.3)   2nd Cons. Rd. @ Hillman Rd.   4.2 (6.8)
Turn East on to 2nd Cons. Rd.

34.3 (55.2)   CK 1/Lakeshore Dr.   2.4 (3.9)
               @ 2nd Cons Rd.
Turn North on to CK 1/Lakeshore Dr.
CK = Municipality of Chatham-Kent road

36.2 (58.3)   CK 1 @ CK 3/PH 3/Talbot Trail   0.6 (1.0)
Continue traveling East to go to Wheatley Prov. Pk.

36.8 (59.2)   Wheatley Prov. Pk. Rd.   0.0 (0.0)
               @ CK 3/PH 3
Turn on to Wheatley Prov. Pk. Rd. and enter the Park.

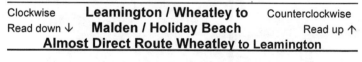

Clockwise	**Leamington / Wheatley to**	Counterclockwise
Read down ↓	**Malden / Holiday Beach**	Read up ↑
	Almost Direct Route Wheatley to Leamington	

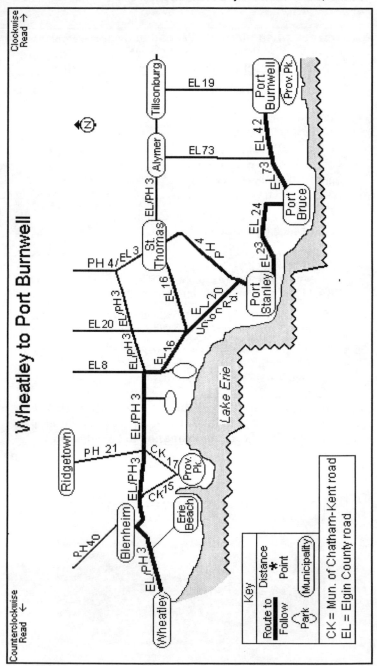

RURAL DELIGHTS

For the next 160 kilometers (100 miles) rich farmland, resort
  towns and friendly people await your presence. It is a wonderful essentially flat ride near the Lake.
This is the heartland of Ontario's farming region. Vegetable and
  fruit farms coexist with dairy cattle. Farm stands dot the route.
Escapees from huge urban areas will marvel at the encompassing
  silence. The cars and trucks on the road will seem quieter
  and perhaps they are quieter.
What do you do when riding with such sensuous richness surrounding you? You think! It's a time to imagine what can and
  will be. It's a time to formulate plans. It's a time to clear your
  mind of all those items that compelled you to bicycle tour. It's
  a true vacation from the daily rigors of surviving in the 21st
  century.
It's also the adventure of going a different way.
Here on the Southeastern Peninsula of Ontario you can wander
  between the fields and really not get lost. It's a grid pattern of
  roads! If you have a moment to wander, then do so.
Most of the automobile traffic speeds along far north of the Lake
  on the 401 expressway. The roads along the shore are yours.

Clockwise	**Wheatley to**	Counterclockwise
Read down ↓	**Dutton**	Read up ↑

0.0 (0.0)   CK 1/Erie St./Wheatley Rd.   66.0 (106.2)
                   @ CK 3/Talbot Trail
Travel East on CK 3/Talbot Trail.
Wheatley information is in the Malden to Wheatley
segment.

26.6 (42.8)   CK 10 @ CK 3/Talbot Trail   39.4 (63.4)
Continue traveling on CK 3/Talbot Trail or turn South on to
CK 10/Towanda Blvd./Erie Shore Dr. to go to Erie Beach
and Erieau.
ERIEAU: **Lodging:** Camping: Bayside Fishing Camp,
PO Box 118, 676-8372; Mariner's Trailer Pk., 825
Mariners Rd.; Molly & O J's, Mariners Rd., 676-8812

30.6 (49.2)   CK 11/Chatham St. @ CK 3   35.4 (57.0)
Continue on CK 3. Turn South on to CK 11, towards
Shrewsbury, to go to Rondeau Prov. Pk. Chatham St. is
termed Communication Rd. in Shrewsbury. It is bit
shorter using CK 11 to CK 15/17 than using CK 3.
BLENHEIM: **Lodging:** Motel. B&Bs: Kelly's Anchor

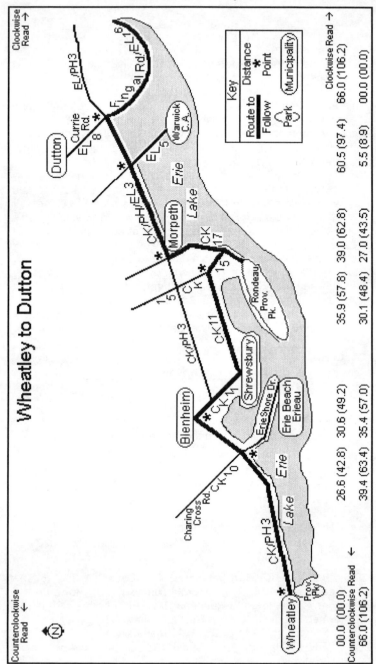

Wheatley to Dutton

Inn, RR 3, 676-1461; Ridge Farms, 12061 Front Line, 674-5934; Stonegate, 776 Hwy. 3, 825-3113.

35.9 (57.8)   CK 15/Bridge Rd. @ CK 3   30.1 (48.4)
Through travelers continue traveling on CK 3/Talbot Trail. The Park entrance is about 5.8 km. (3.6 mi.) from CK 3. Take a lunch break at Rondeau Prov. Pk.! Stay for the night there at the Park or at the private campgrounds near the Rondeau.
MORPETH: **Lodging:** B&Bs: Me-an-ter Inn, 18132 6th Ave., RR 1, 674-1857;Morrison Manor, 18288 Kent Bridge Rd., RR 1, 674-3431. Camping: Rondeau Prov. Pk., Kent Rd. 51, 674-5405; Rondeau Shores Trail. Pk., CR 17, 674-3330; The Summer Place Marina & Cpgd., 18254 Kent Bridge Rd., 674-2326; Wildwood by the Lake, 12443 Rose Beach Ln., 674-5516.

39.0 (62.8)   CK 17 @ CK 3/Talbot Line   27.0 (43.5)
Eastern entrance road for Rondeau Prov. Pk.

59.0 (94.9)   EL 76/Graham Rd. @ EL 3   7.0 (11.3)
Continue East on EL 3. Eagle

60.5 (97.4)   Warwick Consv. Area @ EL 3   5.5 (8.9)
Turn South Dunborough Rd. to go to Warwick Conservation Area (camping).

66.0 (106.2)   EL 8/Currie Rd.   0.0 (0.0)
                        @ EL 3/Talbot Line
Turn North to go to Dutton.
Turn South to go to Port Stanley.
DUTTON: **Lodging:** B&B: Dunwich Farm, 28620 Marsh Line, 762-3006.

Clockwise	**Dutton to**	Counterclockwise
Read down ↓	**Wheatley**	Read up ↑

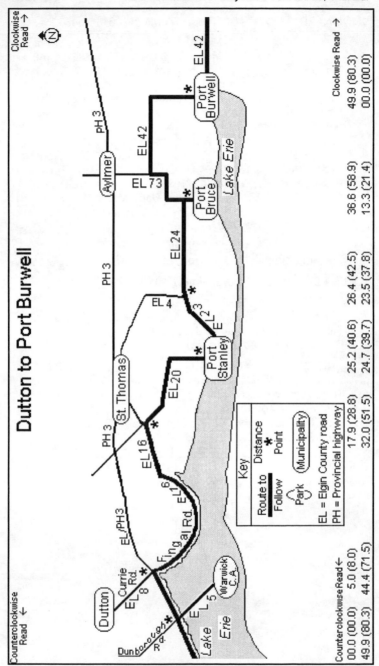

Dutton to Port Burwell

WHAT FUN!

Nothing more than a good ride through small towns and countryside.

Clockwise Read down ↓	Dutton to Port Burwell	Counterclockwise Read up ↑

0.0 (0.0)   Dunborough Rd. @ EL 3   **49.9 (80.3)**
Turn East on to EL 3 to continue traveling clockwise
around Lake Erie.
Turn West on to EL 3 to continue traveling
counterclockwise around the Lake.
Dutton information is in the Wheatley to Dutton segment.

5.5 (8.9)   EL 8/Currie Rd.   **44.4 (71.5)**
              @ EL 3/Talbot Line
Turn South on to EL 8. Turn North to go to Dutton.

6.3 (10.1)   EL 16/Fingal Line   **43.6 (70.2)**
              @ EL 8/Currie Rd.
Turn East on to EL 16/Fingal Line.
John E. Pearce Provincial Park, day use only, is 1.7 mi.
(2.8 km.) South on EL 8. The nearest campground is at
Warwick Conservation Area, 6.3 mi. (10.1 km.) Northeast
of this point on the route.

17.9 (28.8)   EL 20/Union Rd.   **32.0 (51.5)**
              @ EL 16/Fingal Line
Turn South on to EL 20/Union Rd.
Continuing East on EL 16 will bring you to St. Thomas.

ST THOMAS

Info.: St. Thomas-Elgin Tourist Assoc., 631-8188; St.
Thomas ON. Municipality of Central Elgin, 450 Sunset
Dr., St. Thomas ON N5R 5V1, 519 631-4860. AC: 519.
PC: various.
Services: All.
Attractions: Elgin County Railway Mus., 255 Wellington
St., 637-6284; Elgin Military Mus., 30 Talbot St., 633-
7641; St. Thomas-Elgin Public Art Ctr. (STEPAC), 301
Talbot St., 631-4040; Elgin County Pioneer Mus., 32
Talbot St., 631-6537; Kettle Creek Cons. Auth., 44015
Ferguson Line, 631-1270;CASO Elgin County Trans
Canada Trail, PO Box 20006, St. Thomas ON N5P 1Y8;
Meadow Lane Winery, RR 3, 633-1933.
Lodging: Motel. Rosebery Place B&B, 57 Walnut St.,

631-1525; Camping: Dalewood Cons. Area, Dalewood
Dr., 631-1009.

25.2 (40.6)   EL 4/23 @ EL 20   24.7 (39.7)
Turn North on to EL 23.
Port Stanley Conservation Area, day use only.

PORT STANLEY

Services: Restaurants, stores.
Attractions: Port Stanley Festival Theatre, 216 Joseph
St., 782-4353; Port Stanley Terminal Rail, Bridge St./Hwy
4, 782-3730.
Lodging: B&Bs.: Inn on the Harbour, 202 Main St., 782-
7623; On the Beach, 201 William St., 782-3791; Kettle
Creek Inn, 216 Joseph St., 782-3388; Mulberry Lane,
6324 Colborn Rd., 637-4499.

26.4 (42.5)   EL 24 @ EL 23   23.5 (37.8)
Turn East on to EL 24.

36.6 (58.9)   EL 73 @ EL 24   13.3 (21.4)
Turn North on to EL 73 to continue on the route around
Lake Erie. Turn South on to EL 73 to go into Port Bruce
& Port Bruce Prov. Park.
PORT BRUCE: **Lodging:** Camping: Bee-Lin Trailer
Pk., EL 24, 519 773-8092; JR's Beach Trailer Pk., Hwy
73, 519 773-8082.

39.4 (63.4)   EL 42 @ EL 73   10.5 (16.9)
Turn East on to EL 42.

49.1 (79.0)   EL 43 @ EL 42   0.8 (1.3)
Continue East on EL 42
Iroquois Provincial Park

49.9 (80.3)   EL 19 @ EL 42   0.0 (0.0)
PORT BURWELL: **Attractions:** Port Burnwell Marine
Mus., Robinson St., 874-4343. **Lodging:** Camping: Port
Burwell Prov. Pk., 9 Chatham St., 874-4601; Big Otter
Marina & Campground, Hwy 19, 874-4034; Erie Vu, In
town, 874-4673; Sand Hills Pk., RR 2, 586-3891.

Clockwise	**Port Burwell**	Counterclockwise
Read down ↓	**to Dutton**	Read up ↑

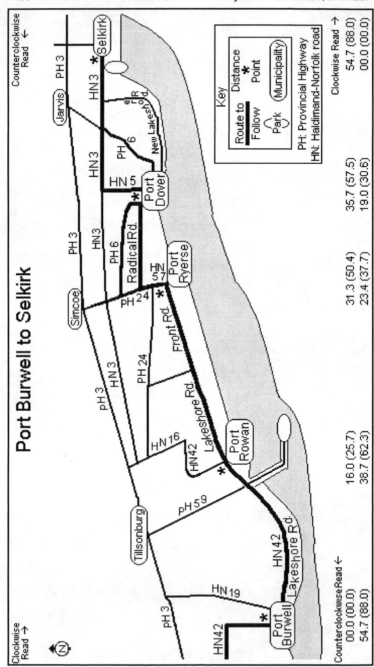

Port Burwell to Selkirk

OTHER CULTURES

The other day I spoke with my sister.

"We just came back from a trip."

"Where did you go this time?" My sister loves to travel. She never learned how to ride a bicycle and thus must use autos or public transit. Her concept of camping is a hotel with a pool. Although she is a superb cook she really likes to experience the local cuisine on her tours.

To her credit she does walk every day.

"Branston, Missouri!" Pronouncing it, *Missouree.*

"Oh, I've never been there. You must have gone for the gambling." I replied with surprise, knowing that neither my sister nor brother-in-law are high rollers.

"There is no gambling in Branston. It prides itself on being a family entertainment community. We went for the shows."

"You, went for the country-western music?"

"No, they have all types of musical/variety shows. We saw 9 shows in 7 days. We had a good time and only one show was just O. K."

You have to remember that my sister lives in the New York City metropolitan area and sees a Broadway/off-Broadway show every few weeks. For New York City area folks there is no *culture* west of the Hudson River and north of the Bronx, and the Atlantic Ocean is east of the *City*.

Her last statement was a testament to having a good time enjoying *quality culture*.

"You know we've done quite a lot of traveling but Branston was so different. I don't think I've ever been in such a different culture!"

I laughed and laughed. "You didn't have to leave North America to experience an exotic culture. Now you know why folks from the mid-west visit New York City—to experience an exotic culture!"

Cultural differences are only outward manifestations of adaptations to geographic conditions. It's all in your mind!

Travel helps to destroy the socio-centric stereotypes on which a person's value system is based.

Clockwise	**Port Burwell**	Counterclockwise
Read down ↓	**to Selkirk**	Read up ↑

0.0 (0.0)   EL 19 @ EL 42   54.7 (88.0)
Continue East on CR 42/Lakeshore Rd.
Port Burwell information is in the Dutton to Port Burwell
segment.

15.0 (24.1)   PH 59/Long Pt. Rd.   39.7 (63.9)
                   @ Lakeshore Rd.
                   @ HN 42
Eastbound through cyclists continue East on Lakeshore
Rd. HN 42 turns North here.
Turn South on to PH 59, and travel for 4.9 mi. (8 km.)
along a peninsula to reach Long Point Prov. Pk.

16.0 (25.7)   Lakeshore Rd. @ Pt. Rowan Rd.   38.7 (62.3)
Continue traveling on Lakeshore Rd. Backus Heritage
Village (camping).

PORT ROWAN

Info.: Long Point Country CofC, Port Rowan ON N0E
1M0, 866 281-1416, AC: 519.
Attraction: Long Point Bird Observatory, PO Box 160.
Lodging: B&Bs: Bird I View, RR 3, 586-3258; Abigail's,
1056 Main St., 586-8777; Bayview, 45 Wolven St., 586-
3413; Birds I View, HN 42 (4km W) RR 1, 586-3258.
Camping: Long Point Prov. Pk., PH 59, PO Box 99, 586-
2133; Marina Shores Ltd., PH 59, RR 3, 586-2791;
Norm's Bayview Marina, RR 3, 586-2241; Backus
Heritage Cons. Area, HN 42 & 2nd Concession Rd., 586-
2201.

24.3 (39.1)   Front Rd. @ Lakeshore Rd.   30.4 (48.9)
The road's the same the name's different.   Here, at
Turkey Point Prov. Pk., this road along Erie's lake front
changes its name from Lakeshore Rd. (westward) to
Front Rd. (eastward). **Info.:** Turkey Point Dist. Bus.
Assoc., Turkey Point ON N0E 1T0, 519 426-3288.
Lodging: Camping: Turkey Point Prov. Pk., PO Box 5,
Turkey Point ON N0E 1T0, 426-3239.

30.3 (48.8)   Norfork Consv. Area @ Front Rd.   24.4 (39.3)
Continue traveling on Front Rd.

31.3 (50.4)   HN 57 @ Front Rd.   23.4 (37.7)
   Turn North on to Pt. Ryerse Rd., then East on to Radical
   Rd./Pt. Dover Rd. We are talking .1 mi. (.2 km.) Follow
   the signs to Port Dover Rd.
   SIMCOE: **Info.:** Simcoe & Dist. CofC, 76 Kent St. S.,
   Simcoe ON N3Y 2Y1, 519 426-5867. AC 519. PC:
   various. **Lodging:** Motel. B&B: Appletree House, 1837
   St. Johns Rd., 426-1828; Country Doll House, 329 Conc.
   14, 426-6826; Longland Farm, St. John's Rd. E., 426-
   7471; Red Door, 481 Norfolk St. S., 426-1605.

32.7 (52.6)   Hay Creek Consv. Area   22.0 (35.4)
                   @ Port Dover Rd.
   Camping, 428-1466,\.

35.7 (57.5)   Port Dover Rd./Radical Rd.   19.0 (30.6)
                   @ PH 6/HN 5
   Turn Northeast on to HN 5/Chapman St.
   Note that PH 6 intersects Port Dover Rd./Radical Rd./
   Talbot Trail Historic Route and that CR 5/Chapman St.
   (in Pt. Dover) intersects PH 6/Main St.

PORT DOVER
Info.: Port Dover Bd. of Trade, 17 Market St. W., Port
Dover ON N0A 1N0, 519 583-1314. AC: 519.
Attractions: Lighthouse Festival Theatre, Main & Market
Sts., PO Box 1208, 583-2221; Port Dover Harbour Mus.,
44 Harbour St., 583-2660.
Lodging: Motels & hotel. B&Bs: Lakeshore Manor, 168
New Lakeshore Rd., 583-2205; Selmer Haus, 244 St.
George St., 583-0729; B&B By The Lake, 30 Elm Park,

583-1010; By The Lake, 30 Elm Pk., 583-1010; Clonmel
Estate, 11 Mill Rd., 583-0519; Peggy Jane's, 49 John St.,
583-1636; Port of Call, 602 Main St., 583-1642;
Woodhouse Lodge, RR 1, 428-1717; Frames by Forrest,
2008 Park St., 583-3518; Lakeshore Manor, 168 New
Lakeshore Dr., 583-2205. Camping: Hay Creek Cons.
Area, Pt. Ryerse Rd. & Radical Rd., 428-1466; Shore
Acres Pk., Nelson St. W., 583-2222.

39.7 (63.9)   HN 3 @ HN 5   15.0 (24.1)
Turn East on to HN 3. A bit further North (5 km. (3.1 mi.))
and parallel to HN 3 is PH 3. PH 3 is a major east-west
road with wider lanes and shoulders than HN 3. You can
bicycle on PH 3.

45.8 (73.7)   Nanticoke Village @ HN 3   8.9 (14.3)
Continue East on HN 3.
NANTICOKE: Lodging: Shadow Lawn, RR 1,
   776-0347

50.0 (80.5)   HN 18 @ HN 3   4.7 (7.6)
Continue East on HN 3.
Tired? I doubt it! Turn South, towards Lake Erie to go to
Haldimand Conservation Area. Return to HN 3 by going
East on Lakeshore Rd. then turning North on to HN 62.

53.1 (85.5)   Park Rd. @ HN 3   1.6 (2.6)
Continue East on HN 3 to go to Selkirk.
Turn South on to Park Rd. for 1.6 km (1 mi.) to go to
Selkirk Provincial Park.

54.7 (88.0)   HN 53 @ HN 3   0.0 (0.0)

SELKIRK

Info.: Selkirk CofC, PO Box 275, Selkirk ON N0A 1P0,
905 776-2627. AC: 905. PC: N0A 1P0.
Attraction: Canadian Drilling Rig Mus., RR 3 & RR 8,
776-0919; Cottonwood Mansion, 740 Reg. Rd. 53, 776-
2538; Wilson MacDonald School Mus., Cheapside &
Rainham Rds., 776-3319.
Lodging: Broomtree Guest House, 205 E. Lakeshore
Rd., 776-1846. Camping: Haldimand Cons. Area, 645 W.
Lakeshore Rd., RR 3776-2700; Selkirk Prov. Pk., Reg.
Rd. 3, RR 1, 776-2600.

Clockwise	**Selkirk to**	Counterclockwise
Read down ↓	**Port Burwell**	Read up ↑

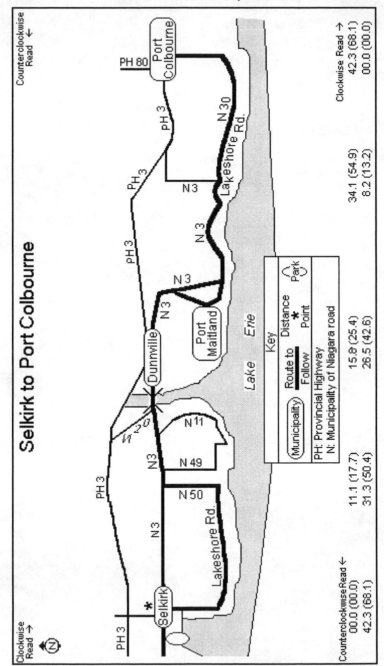

Selkirk to Port Colbourne

RESORTS AND MORE

Along the lake's shore, in the midst of this beautiful countryside, are a series of resort communities. Devoid of theme parks and arcade type attractions these hamlets and villages mainly serve as oases for boaters and visitors seeking relief from urban summer heat. Demure and lively at the same time, each of the resort villages along Lake Erie's northern shore has its own character.

Some villages and cities are *intellectual* in nature, with resident theatre companies and well known visual arts communities. Other towns are simply places to have a summer cottage or enjoy the beach for a day or two. Take some time to go to the most local of the restaurants and taverns to engage a resident in conversation.

Clockwise Read down ↓	Selkirk to Port Colborne	Counterclockwise Read up ↑
0.0 (0.0)	HN 53 @ HN 3	42.3 (68.1)

Turn Southeast on HN 53 in Selkirk. Lakeshore Rd. makes a zig zag turn here to cross the bridge. HN 3 is parallel to and ~.8 km. (.5 mi.) from Lakeshore Rd.
SELKIRK: Selkirk information is in the Port Burwell to Selkirk segment.

1.0 (1.6)	Lakeshore Rd. @ HN 53	41.3 (66.5)

Turn East on to Lakeshore Rd.

11.0 (17.7)	HN 50 @ Lakeshore Rd.	31.3 (50.4)

Continue East on Lakeshore Rd.

12.2 (19.6)	HN 3 @ CR 50	30.1 (48.4)

Turn East on to CR 3.

14.6 (23.5)	HN 49 @ HN 3	27.7 (44.6)

Through cyclists continue riding East on HN 3
OR take a scenic route by turning South (towards the Lake) on to HN 49. At Lake Erie turn East and travel along Old Lakeshore Rd. to the Grand River. At the River turn North on HN 11 to return to HN 3. You can not cross the Grand River at it's mouth! This route, going through Port Maitland, is a bit longer, ~10.0 km. (6.2 mi.), but the scenery is also a bit nicer.

15.8 (25.4)	HN 20/11 @ HN 3	26.5 (42.6)

Through travelers cross the Grand River bridge and

continue traveling East on CR 3 into Dunnville. Tired
bicyclists can camp in this area. BYNG: Byng Is. Cons.
Area, 9 Haldimand Trail/Cty Rd. 11, 774-5755.
Turn North on to Rt. 20 to go to Byng Island
Conservation Area (camping). PH 3 is only a block
north of CR 3 at this point along the route. If you want to
avoid the more leisurely pace of CR 3 then use PH 3.

DUNNVILLE
Info.: Dunnville CofC, 222 Lock St. W., Dunnville ON
N1A 2X1 905 774-3183.
Lodging: Motels. B&Bs: Lalor Estate Inn, 241 Broad St.
W., 774-5438; Pat & Pat's, 125 RR 65, Hutchinson Rd.,
899-1054; Sleep Inn, 448 RR 17, 774-8502; Sleep Inn,
448 RR 117, 774-8502; Waltham's Way, 308 Alder St.
E., 774-6174; Betamik Harbour, 776 Main St. E., 774-
5372; Century Home, 310 Helena St., 774-5724; Inn
Over Our Heads, 237 Lakeshore Rd., 774-4473; Sunset
Shore, 512 Main St. W., 774-5840; Camping: Byng Is.
Cons. Area, 9 Haldimand Trail/Cty Rd. 11, 774-5755;
Knight's Beach, 2190 Lakeshore Rd., 774-4566; Rock
Point Prov. Pk., 215 Niece Rd., 774-6642.

17.4 (28.0)   PH 3/HN 17 @ HN 3   24.9 (40.1)
Continue East on HN 3.
About 11.0 km. (7 mi.) from this intersection in
Lowbanks hamlet there are a few campgrounds. They
are not listed in any directories but they do exist.

17.9 (28.8)   PH 3 @ HN 3   24.4 (39.3)
Continue traveling on HN 3 which is the scenic *by the
shore* route. PH 3 does have a wide shoulder and is a
bit straighter. PH 3 & HN 3 intersect again at Port
Colborne.
Rock Pt. Prov. Pk. (camping) is approximately 8 km. (5
mi.) from this intersection. Long Beach Conservation
Area is about 8 km. (5 mi.) East of Rock Pt. along HN 3.
Long Beach is the first/last gov't. entity campground
from the Niagara River.

34.1 (54.9)   N 30/Lakeshore Rd. @ N 3   8.2 (13.2)
Continue East on HN 30/Lakeshore Rd. HN 3 turns
North at this point and junctions with PH 3 in about 1.9
km. (1.2 mi.). You can take either HN 3/PH 3 or
Lakeshore Rd./HN 3 into Port Colborne. The distance
is about the same only the scenery is changed to
protect the bicyclist's eyes. BURNABY

40.8 (65.7)   PH 80 @ Lakeshore Rd./N 30   1.5 (2.4)
Turn North on to PH 80.

42.3 (68.1)   PH 3 @ N 80   0.0 (0.0)

PORT COLBORNE

Info.: Port Colborne Tourism, 66 Charlotte St., Port Colborne ON L3K 3C8, 905 835-2900.
Lighthouse Info. Booth, Welland Canal, 22 Main St. W, 905 834-5722. AC: 905. PC: various.
Attraction: Showboat Festival Theatre, 296 Fielden Ave., 834-0833; Caudière Navigation, 201 West St., 834-1536; Port Colborne Marine Mus., 280 King St., 834-7604; Fountain View Pk - Lock 8, Welland Canal, 22 Main St. W, 834-5722.
Lodging: Motels. B&Bs: Kent House, 115 Kent St., 834-1206; Ingleside, 322 King St., 835-5062; King George Inn, 239 King St., 834-8096; Long Beach, 25 L 67 Lakeshore Rd., 899-0566. Camping: Sherkston Shores, 490 Empire Rd., RR 1, 894-0972.

Clockwise	**Port Colborne**	Counterclockwise
Read down ↓	**to Selkirk**	Read up ↑

Welland Canal - Pt. Colborne to Welland

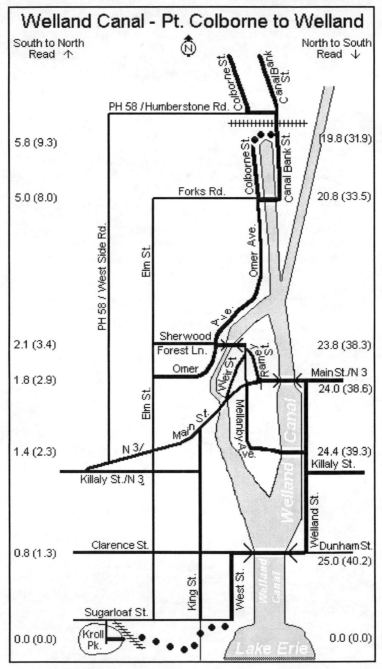

South to North
Read ↑

North to South
Read ↓

WELLAND CANAL
THE MERRITT TRAIL

The first time I bicycled across the Niagara Peninsula from St. Catharines to Pt. Colborne was after helping Ray Howe transport his trimaran *Earth Voyager* through the Welland Canal. We had to motor the *Earth Voyager* on the waterway from Pt. Colborne to St. Catharines. Then Bob Howe (Ray's brother) and I took our bicycles off the trimaran and began to bike south from Port Dalhouise on Lake Ontario.

It was late in the day when we started out and by the time we reached Thorold dusk was upon us. There was still enough fading day light for us to make our way to Beaverdams Rd. My 2.5 watt front light lead the way; my back red flashing light was easy for Bob to follow. The front light certainly wasn't strong enough but it was the only light I brought with me. I really didn't expect us to be riding after sundown but a stuck lock delayed our passage through the Canal. The headlight depleted its battery power just as the sun dipped below the horizon. I had no spare batteries and it was a mid-summer moonless night. With no bicycle lights we somehow followed the automobile lit shoulder.

At Beaverdams Rd. we turned south on to PH 406, which as a 400 series road does not permit bicycles on the roadway or shoulder (gravel). Onward we slugged. I couldn't understand why all those cars were honking at us!

Frequently Bob would come within earshot of me and say, "I think we're on the wrong road."

"Naw. We're going the right way," I'd shout back.

From time to time, in the 1 candlepower brilliance of my front light and the flashing headlights of passing cars, I'd pull out the "official" map of the *Merritt Trail* to check our progress.

Finally I relented. At Port Robinson Road we left the 406 and made our way to Merrittville Road. Southward we continued. It had taken an interminable amount of time to cover the distance on from Thorold to Pt. Robinson. This was due to the gravel shoulder and the fear of being destroyed by fast moving autos that could barely discern our outline in the darkness. Most of the drivers must have known we were crazy.

The *Merritt Trail* is not a continuous off road trail at this point in time. Like so many other trails in Canada and the United States it is a *work in progress*. Money, bureaucratic commitment and citizen advocacy are the crucial elements for completing bicyclist and pedestrian off road facilities. It takes a committed group of citizens to cajole and annoy government officials to commit the funds necessary to complete these trails. The Merritt Trail is just one example of a partially finished off road trail.

The major problem with *incomplete* trails is that they are built in a discontinuous fashion. Political expediency usually takes precedence over practical travel situations. Unlike roadways, trials are constructed opportunistically. This means that where a right of way exists that does not entail land purchases the trail is built. It matters little to the political powers that the 1, 2 or 5 mile/kilometer section does not connect with any other section of the trail.

"When we have the funds, we'll acquire the land and build the rest of the trail," the politicians and bureaucrats state. They continue their litany by saying, "in the mean time you have a nice recreational trail in this area."

By diminishing the importance of longer off road trails for bicyclist and pedestrian use; by not completing trails/on road facilities the politicians; bureaucrats and citizen automobile devotees create a situation which only leads to more dependence on personal motorized forms of travel.

I'm really not in favor of off road trails. I believe that a much less expensive and more useful way of encouraging bicycle and pedestrian use is the development of on road lanes/ shoulders. We cannot expect folks to go a ½ mile out of their way to travel 1½ miles to a store. A wide paved shoulder is a much more efficient and useful way to encourage people to move their muscles.

Unique natural and man made structures such as the Welland Canal deserve to have a parallel off road trail so that folks can observe its usefulness and drink in its scenic beauty. A completed *Merritt Trail* would provide an efficient means to connect the cities along the Canal from Lake to Lake. Combine that with a bus system to transport folks back to their starting point from either end of the *Trail* and a mighty fine tourist attraction is created for urban outdoor adventurers!

South to North	**Port Colborne**	North to South
Read down ↓	**to St. Catharines**	Read up ↑

Welland Canal Route Lake Erie to Lake Ontario

0.0 (0.0)   H H Kroll Lakeside Pk./Welland Trail   25.8 (41.5)
@ Sugarloaf St.
You are standing inside the park near the entrance. Look towards the railway tracks, find the entrance to the trail across the tracks near the apartment building. You could use Sugarloaf St. but it is narrow. West bound 'round the Lakers turn West on to Sugarloaf St.

0.3 (0.5)   West St. @ Welland Trail/Sugarloaf St.   25.5 (41.0)
Turn North on to the levee or West St./Welland Trail.

0.7 (1.1)   Harbourfront Lift Bridge/Clarence St.   25.1 (40.4)
@ West St
Turn East on to the Harbourfront Bridge & cross the Welland Canal. Alternatively turn West, go 1 block to King St. and turn North onto King St. This alternative route will join the main route .9 mi. (1.8 km.)

0.8 (1.3)   Harbourfront Lift Bridge   25.0 (40.2)
@ Welland St./Dunham St.
Turn North on to Welland St. Turning South on Welland St. to go to Nickel Beach Pk. (swimming). Traveling East on Dunham St. will take you along the Lake Erie shore but its a circuitous route along narrow and sometimes not the finest cottage roads.

1.1 (1.8)   Welland St. @ Killaly St.   24.7 (39.7)
East bound cyclists turn East here on to Killaly St. and follow the route to Ft. Erie

1.4 (2.3)   Mellanby Ave. @ Welland St.   24.4 (39.3)
Continue traveling North on Welland St. Turning West on to Mellanby Ave. & crossing the Canal

1.8 (2.9)   Main St. East/N 3/PH 3 @ Welland St.   24.0 (38.6)
Turn West on to the Main St. lift bridge. Less than 1 yd. (1 m.) from the Northwest corner of this Main St. lift Bridge is Ramey Ave. It is directly opposite the Chamber of Commerce "Windmill" tourism kiosk and Lock 8 Park. Turn North on to Ramey Ave. You might be wondering if I'm nuts. I'm not, actually you'll be rewarded with a very interesting way of crossing the Welland Canal. If you miss Ramey St. continue traveling West on Main St. W. to Elm St. (.5 mi./.8 km.) and then turn North on Elm St.

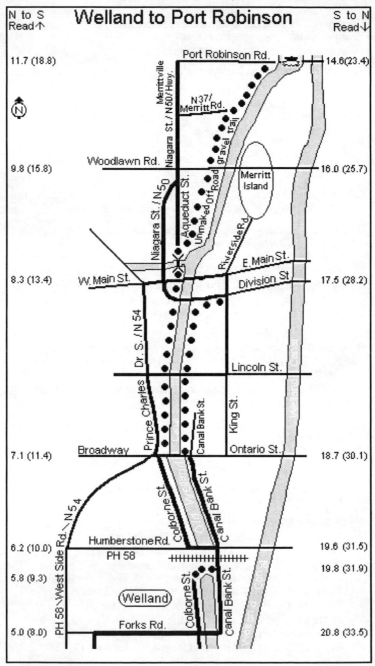

Welland to Port Robinson

2.0 (3.2)   Ramey Ave. @ Weir St.   23.8 (38.3)
Yikes! Ramey Ave. ends at what looks like the end of the
earth! Look North! See the foot bridge. Cross it and go to
Omer Ave.

2.1 (3.4)   Foot bridge @ Omer Ave.   23.7 (38.1)
Either turn North on to Omer St. The route follows an off
road trail for 2.9 mi. (4.7 km.) to Forks Rd. Or turn South
on to Omer Ave. for .5 mi. (.8 km.) then turn North on
Elm St. for 3.2 mi. (5.1 km.) to Fork Rd. You are actually
traveling parallel to the Old Welland Canal.

5.0 (8.0)   Omer Ave./Elm St. @ Fork Rd.   20.8 (33.5)
If you've been traveling on Omer Ave., cross Fork Rd. to
Colborne St. If you traveled on Elm St. turn East and
then North on to Colborne St. This is a Park area. Read
the next entry & decide if you want to go across the field
or simply want to keep going East across the Old Welland Canal to Canal Bank St. on the East bank of the Old
Canal.

5.8 (9.3)   End of Colborne St.   20.0 (32.2)
                @ S. Niagara Rowing Clubhouse
Turn East & look for the path which goes around the top
of the Old Welland Canal to Canal Bank St. It will actually
appear as if you'll be traveling through a field which you
will be doing.

6.0 (9.7)   Path @ Canal Bank St.   19.8 (31.9)
Amazingly you negotiated the trail & are now standing on
the Canal Bank St. roadway. Ride North on Canal Bank
Rd. Yeah, you could have simply traveled North on Canal Bank St. from Colborne Rd. to Humberstone Rd. but
wasn't it fun to go off road a bit!

6.2 (10.0)   Canal Bank Rd. @   19.6 (31.5)
               Humberstone Rd./Townline Tunnel Rd./PH 58
Travel North on either Canal Bank Rd. or Colborne Rd.
There is a paved path along the Old Canal parallel to Ca-
nal Bank Rd. Both Roads exit on to Ontario St.

7.1 (11.4)   Canal Bank Rd./Colborne Rd.   18.7 (30.1)
               @ Ontario Rd.
The west side (Colborne Rd.) route becomes an off road
trail exiting at Lincoln St. (.6 mi./1.0 km.) and at W. Main
St. (1.2 mi./1.9 km.) north of Ontario St. The east side
route travels for a short distance on Canal Bank St. and
then turns into an off road trail through a park along the

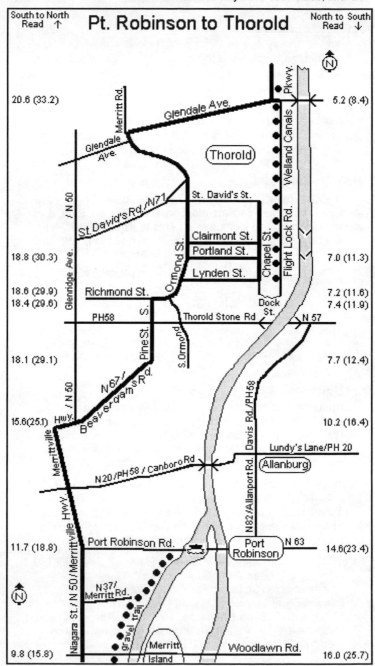

Pt. Robinson to Thorold

Welland Recreational Waterway.

8.3 (13.4)   Division St./Main St.   17.5 (28.2)
               @ Trail/King St./Niagara St.
West side Route: Turn East on to Division St. you'll be
crossing the Canal. At King St. Turn North and then West
on to Main St. Yeah, you've gone around in circles! Just
after crossing again the Rec. Waterway, go on to the
sidewalk and you'll be at an entrance to a trial. It is a very
obscure, overgrown entrance. East Side Route: Exit the
trail at King St. @ Division St. Travel due North on King
St., crossing Main St. & cycle on to Riverside St. into
Merritt Is. Park. Both of these trails exit on to Woodlawn
Rd. , 1.6 mi./2.5 km. North of Main St. It is the same distance to Woodlawn Rd. no matter which route you use.
WELLAND

Note
Alternate Road Rt. due to obscurity of trail: West side:
Continue traveling west to Niagara St./N 50. This is a
busy street, It does have a paved on roadway shoulder &
a sidewalk but there are many store driveways. East
side: ride East on Division St. to Burger St. Turn North on
Burger St. riding across Main St. E. on to River Rd.
Travel North on River Rd. to Woodlawn Rd.

9.8 (15.8)   Woodlawn Rd.   16.0 (25.7)
               @ Niagara St./River Rd./Merritt Is. Pk. Trail/
               @ West Bank Trail
Trail riders & those on River Rd.: turn West on to Woodlawn Rd. and ride to Niagara St. (between .4 & .9 mi./.6 &
1.4 km.). Turn North on to Niagara St. The West side trail
continues North to the "missing bridge" at Allenburg but
is a barely a gravel path in many places.

11.1 (17.9)   Niagara St./Merrittville Rd./N 50   14.7(23.7)
               @ Merritt Rd./N 37
Continue traveling North on Merrittville Rd. Simply a
name change Niagara St. = Merrittville Rd. both are N
50.

13.1 (21.1)   Merrittville Rd./N 50   12.7 (20.4)
               @ Canboro Rd./N 20
Traveling East on Canboro Rd./N 20 will bring you to Niagara Falls. After carefully crossing PH 406 (no bikes
allowed) N 20 jct. with PH 58 eventually becoming
Lundy's Lane/N 20/PH 58 going into the Falls.

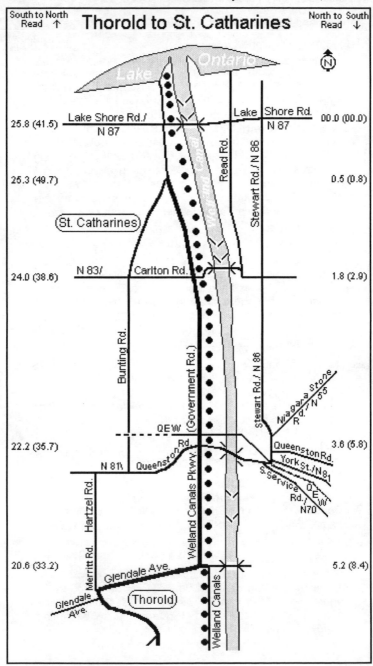

Thorold to St. Catharines

Lake Ontario

25.8 (41.5) — Lake Shore Rd./ N 87 — Lake Shore Rd. / N 87 — 00.0 (00.0)

Welland Canal

Read Rd.

Stewart Rd./ N 86

25.3 (49.7) — 0.5 (0.8)

St. Catharines

24.0 (38.6) — N 83/ Carlton Rd. — 1.8 (2.9)

Bunting Rd.

(Government Rd.)

Stewart Rd./ N 86

Niagara Stone Rd./ N 55

QEW

22.2 (35.7) — Queenston Rd. — 3.6 (5.8)

QueenstonRd.

N 81\ Queenston Rd.

York St./N 81

S. Service

Welland Canals Pkwy.

QEW Rd./ N70

Hartzel Rd.

Merritt Rd.

20.6 (33.2) — Glendale Ave. — 5.2 (8.4)

Glendale Ave.

Thorold

Welland Canals

15.6 (25.1)   Merrittville Rd./N 50   10.2 (16.4)
                @ Beaverdams Rd./N 67
Turn Northeast on to Beaverdams Rd./N 67.

18.1 (29.1)   Beaverdams Rd./N 67 @ Pine St. S.   7.7 (12.4)
Turn North on to Pine St. S. You will start to see signs
leading to Lock 7.

18.4 (29.6)   Pine St. @ Richmond St.   7.4 (11.9)
Turn East on to Richmond St. If you miss Richmond St.
continue North to Sullivan St. & then turn East.

18.6 (29.9)   Richmond St. @ Ormond St.   7.2 (11.6)
Turn North on to Ormond St. Actually you have no choice
because Richmond bends into Ormond. There will be
signs directing you to Lock 7.

18.8 (30.3)   Ormond St. @ Portland Ave.   7.0 (11.3)
Turn East on to Portland Ave. If you miss this side street
continue traveling north on Ormond St. which changes
its name to Merritt St. and finally intersects with Glendale
Ave./N 89. Turning East on to Glendale Ave./N 89 will
bring you to the Welland Canal/Canal (off road) Trail/
Welland Canals Pkwy. (Government Rd.)

19.0 (30.6)   Portland Ave.   6.8 (10.9)
                @ Flight Lock Rd./Lock 7
Go down to the Lock & look for the Flight Lock Rd. Trail.
Turn North on the Trail.

20.6 (33.2)   Flight Lock Rd. Trail   5.2 (8.4)
                @ Glendale Rd./N 89
Cross Glendale Rd./N 89 and continue traveling North on
the off road asphalt paved Trail which parallels the Canal. You'll pass Locks 7-4 and understand why this is
Flight Lock Rd.!

21.4 (34.4)   Lock 3 Welland Canals Center   4.4 (7.1)
                @ Canal Trail
Continue traveling North on the Trail. The Center has
some food service, lavatories and souvenir shops.

22.2 (35.7)   Welland Canals Trail   3.6 (5.8)
                @ Queenston Rd./N 81
Continue traveling North on the Trail. Queenston Rd./N
70 like Glendale Rd./N 89 & other Regional Roads trav-
ersing the Niagara Peninsula east <--> west. Traveling
East from here will bring you into Niagara Falls. Traveling
West on Queenston Rd./N 81 will bring you through the

Peninsula's wine country (marked by grape signs) to Hamilton.
Use Queenston Rd./81 to cross the Canal and then use the the South Service Rd. to Niagara Falls. Traveling Northeast via Niagara Stone Rd./N 55 will bring you to Niagara-on-the-Lake.

24.0 (38.6)   Welland Canals Trail/Lock 2   1.8 (2.9)
                    @ Carlton Rd./N 83
Continue traveling North on the Trail. Like N 55 & N 87/ Lakeshore Rd. further north, traveling East on Carlton Rd. will bring you into Niagara-on-the-Lake.

25.8 (41.5)   Welland Canals Trail/Lock 1   0.0 (0.0)
                    @ Lakeshore Rd./N 87
The Trail continues North, on the west side of the Canal, through Malcolmson Park to Lake Ontario. There is a parallel trail to the Lake on the East side of the Canal. Ontario's Waterfront Trail intersects with the Welland Canals Trail at Lake Ontario on the West side of the Canal; on the East side of the Canal the Waterfront Trail parallels Lakeshore Rd. Note that the Waterfront Trail may not be suitable for bicycling at various points along its right of way.

Clockwise	**St. Catharines**	Counterclockwise
Read down ↓	**to Port Colborne**	Read up ↑

Welland Canal Route Lake Erie to Lake Ontario

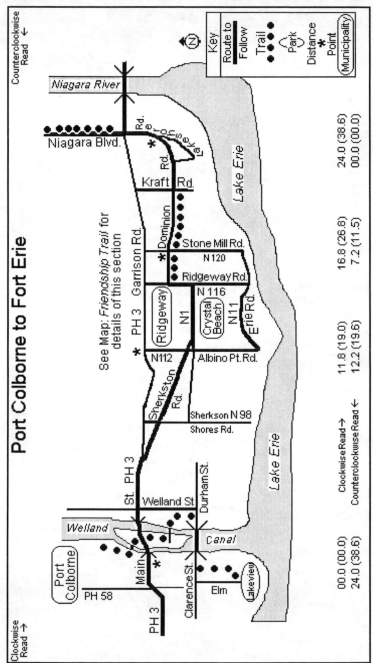

Port Colborne to Fort Erie

Counterclockwise Read ←

Clockwise Read →

Key

Route to Follow

Trail

Park

Distance ✳

Point

(Municipality)

Niagara River

Niagara Blvd.

Lake Erie

Rd.

Kraft Rd.

Dominion Rd.

Stone Mill Rd.

N 120

Garrison Rd.

PH 3

Ridgeway Rd.

N 116

Ridgeway

N1

Crystal Beach

N11

Erie Rd.

N112

Albino Pt. Rd.

Sherkston Rd.

Sherkson Shores Rd.

N 98

St. PH 3

Welland St

Durham St.

Welland

Main

Canal

Lake Erie

Port Colborne

PH 58

Clarence St.

Elm

Lakeview

PH 3

See Map: *Friendship Trail* for details of this section

	Clockwise Read →	Counterclockwise Read ←
	24.0 (38.6)	00.0 (00.0)
	16.8 (26.8)	7.2 (11.5)
	11.8 (19.0)	12.2 (19.6)
	00.0 (00.0)	24.0 (38.6)

Clockwise Read →

Counterclockwise Read ←

AN ELLIPSE HAS NO BEGINNING OR END

If you began this cyclotour in Buffalo, New York then you've completed the ellipse around Lake Erie. You can travel North to Lake Ontario. On your way you can follow the water as it flows from Lake to Lake and over Niagara Falls.

Spend some time marveling at the rejuvenated spirit which is taking hold along the North Coast of the United States and the South Coast of Canada. The residents of the Great Lakes have a different attitude from the 150 or so years when this region was the dominant manufacturing center. It is still a *we can do anything* spirit but now it is tempered by time.

Clockwise Read down ↓	**Port Colborne to Fort Erie**	Counterclockwise Read up ↑
0.0 (0.0)	PH 3 @ PH 80	24.0 (38.6)

Turn East on to PH 3.
Port Colborne information is in the Selkirk to Port Colborne segment.

8.9 (14.3)	N 112 @ PH 3	15.1 (24.3)

Turn South on to N 112. N means Niagara County road.

10.8 (17.4)	N 1 @ N 112	11.2 (18.0)

N 1 is a more direct alternative road to N 11. N 11 weaves along the shore whereas N 1 is basically a straight road.

CRYSTAL BEACH: **Info.:** Crystal Beach Bus. Assoc., PO Box 360, Crystal Beach ON L0S 1B0. **Lodging:** Motels. B&B: Crossroads, 276 Cambridge Rd. W., 894-4161.

11.8 (19.0)	N 11 @ N 112	12.2 (19.6)

Turn East on to N 11.

19.0 (30.6)	N 1 @ N 11	0.5 (0.8)

Turn East on to CR 1

24.0 (38.6)	Peace Bridge @ N 1	0.0 (0.0)

Follow the signs to the Peace Bridge. Hurrah!

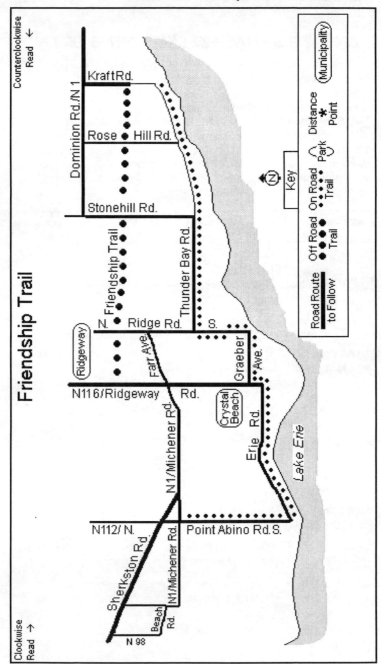

FORT ERIE

Info.: Fort Erie CofC, 660 Garrison Rd., Fort Erie ON L2A 6E2, 905 871-3803.

Services: Bike shop. Bridge: Bicyclists walk their bikes on the walkway or ride on the roadway depending upon vehicle traffic conditions. Buffalo & Fort Erie Public Bridge Auth., 10 Queen St., PO Box 232, 871-1608.

Attractions: Fort Erie Race Track, 230 Catherine St., 871-3200; Fort Erie Friendship Festival, PO Box 1241, 871-6454; Fort Erie Firefighting Mus., 118 Concession Rd., 671-1271; Fort Erie Railroad Mus., Central Ave., 894-5332; Historic Fort Erie, Niagara Pkwy, 871-0540; Mildred M. Mahoney Dolls' House Gallery, 657 Niagara Blvd., 871-5833; Fort Erie Battlefield Mus., Hwy. 3, 894-5332; Fort Erie Hist. Mus., 402 Ridge Rd., 894-5332.

Lodging: Motels. B&Bs: Crescent Park, 969 Buffalo Rd., 871-6747; Fort Erie Niagara Riverview, 21 Cairns Crescent, Serv. Rd. A., 871-0865; River's Edge, 551 Niagara Blvd., 994-7128; Split Rock Farms, 1652 Ridge Rd. N., Ridgeway, 382-7777.

Camping: Knight's Hide-Away Pk., 1154 Gorham Rd., RR 116, 894-1911; Windmill Point Pk., 2409 Dominion Rd., 894-2809.

Clockwise	**Fort Erie to**	Counterclockwise
Read down ↓	**Port Colborne**	Read up ↑

APPENDIX

Contents

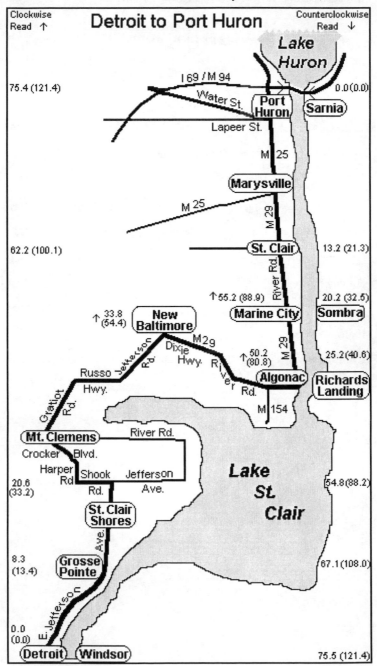

Detroit to Port Huron

LAKE ERIE TO LAKE HURON
USA ROUTE

Clockwise ↓ Read mi. (km.)	**Detroit to Port Huron**	Counterclockwise mi. (km.) Read ↑

Travelers Note: Highway Terminology
State maintained roads in Michigan are termed *M* __.
Highways maintained with the use of United States federal government funds are termed *US* __ or I __.
County maintained roads are abbreviated *CR* __.

0.0 (0.0)   Woodward Ave.   75.4 (121.4)
                         @ E. Jefferson Ave.
Travel East on E. Jefferson Ave.
DETROIT: See River Rouge to Detroit Segment for information.

8.3 (13.4)   E. Jefferson Ave.   67.1 (108.0)
                         @ Lake Shore Dr.
Continue traveling Northeast on Lake Shore Dr.

GROSSE POINTE
Info.: Grosse Pointe, Grosse Pointe Shores & Grosse Pointe Woods. www.thevillagegp.com;
Services: Bike shop in Grosse Pointe Woods. Grocery.
Attraction: Edsel & Eleanor Ford House, 1100 Lake Shore Rd., Grosse Point Shores, 313 884-4222.

12.7 (20.4)   Lake Shore Dr.   62.7 (100.9)
                         @ Jefferson Ave.
Continue traveling on Lake Shore Dr./Jefferson Ave.
The road's name changes as you enter Macomb Co.

16.2 (26.1)   11 Mile Rd. @ Jefferson Ave.   59.2 (95.3)
Continue traveling North on Jefferson Ave.
Info.: City of St. Clair Shores, 27600 Jefferson Cir., St. Clair Shores 48081.

20.6 (33.2)   Shook Rd. @ Jefferson Ave.   54.8 (88.2)
Turn West on to Shook Rd. to go into Mt. Clemens.
Use Jefferson Ave. to go to Metro Beach Park

21.4 (34.5)   Harper Rd. @ Shook Rd.   54.0 (86.9)
Turn North on to Harper Rd.

23.3 (37.5)   Crocker Blvd. @ Harper Rd.   52.1 (83.9)
Turn Northwest on to Crocker Blvd.

24.1 (38.8)   Gratiot Rd.   51.3 (82.6)
                     @ M 3/Crocker Blvd.
Turn North on to Gratiot Rd.

MT. CLEMENS

Info.: Macomb Co. Dep't of Eco. Development, Admin.
Bldg., Mt. Clemens 48043, 810 469-5285.
Services: Grocery & other retail stores.
Attractions: Michigan Transit Mus., Railroad Depot,
463-1863; Macomb Performing Arts Ctr., 44575 Garfield.
Lodging: Motel.

24.3 (39.1)   North River Rd. @ Gratiot Rd.   51.1 (82.3)
Continue traveling on Gratiot Rd.
St. Clair Metro Beach turn off bikers rejoin us here.

26.7 (43.0)   Hall Rd./Russo Hwy.   48.7 (78.4)
                     @ Gratiot Rd.
Turn East on to Hall Rd./Russo Hwy.

28.5 (45.9)   Jefferson Rd. @ Russo Hwy.   46.9 (75.5)
Turn North on to Jefferson Rd.
You're back at the Lake Huron shore line.

33.8 (54.4)   M 29 @ Jefferson Rd.   41.6 (67.0)
Turn East on to M 29.

35.1 (56.5)   County Line Rd.   40.3 (64.9)
                     @ M 29/Green St./Dixie Hwy.
Continue traveling on M 29. M 29 becomes Dixie Hwy.
and then River Rd. going East from New Baltimore.
NEW BALTIMORE: **Lodging:** Motels.

50.2 (80.8)   Algonac St. Pk. @ M 29   25.2 (40.6)
Continue traveling on M. 29/River Rd.
At Algonac, M 29/River Rd. turns North.

ALGONAC

Services: Ferry to Roberts Landing/Walpole Is. ON is
just North of Algonac St. Pk. Use this ferry or the one at
Marine City, 5 mi. (8 km.) north. This ferry has an irregular schedule.

Attractions: Algonac Theater, 810 794-2522.
Lodging: Motels. Camping: Algonac St. Pk., 8732 River Rd., 810 465-2160; River View, M 29, 810 794-0182.

55.2 (88.9)   Plank Rd. @ M 29/River Rd.   20.2 (32.5)
Continue on M 29.

MARINE CITY
Info.: Marine City, 300 Broadway St., Marine City 48039.
Services: Transportation: Ferry to Sombra ON. If you are planning to travel counterclockwise around Lake Huron then cross the St. Clair River via the Marine City-Sombra Ferry or the Algonac-Walpole Is. Ferry. Then use the *Saria to Windsor* segment from Sombra.
Attractions: Museum.
Lodging: Motels. B&B: Heather House, 409 N. Main St., 810 765-3175.

62.2 (100.1)   Rattle Run @ M 29/River Rd.   13.2 (21.3)
Continue traveling on M 29/River Rd.

ST. CLAIR
Attractions: St. Clair Hist. Mus., 308 S. 4th St.
Lodging: Motels. B&Bs: Clairmont House, 147 Brown St., 329-0047; Murphy Inn, 505 Clinton Ave., 329-7118; William Hopkins Manor, 613 N. Riverside, 329-0188.

65.7 (105.8)   M 29 Jct. River Rd.   9.7 (15.6)
Southern Jct. point of River Rd. & M 29.
Either bear towards the Lake on to River Rd.
Or continue traveling on M 29.

68.9 (110.9)   River Rd. Jct. M 29   6.5 (10.5)
Northern Jct. point of River Rd. & M 29.
Either bear towards the Lake on to River Rd.
Or continue traveling on M 29.

69.4 (111.7)   M 29 Jct. M 25   6.0 (9.7)
Clockwise: Continue North bound on M 25.
Counterclockwise:: Continue South bound on M 29.
MARYSVILLE: **Attraction:** Hist. Mus. **Lodging:** Motels.

73.4 (118.2)   Lapeer St. @ M 25/River Rd.   2.0 (3.2)
Continue traveling North to the Blue Water Bridges.
Actually you're in the heart of Port Huron.

Travelers Note

Transportation: Blue Water Bridge, 519 336-2720, www. bwba.org. The rules for having the Bluewater Bridge Authority help you cross the Bridge are: 1. You must be a *bona fide* tourist. 2. You must show a picture identification of your residence. The Authority suggests you use the ferry between Sombra, ON and Marine City, MI which is ~20mi. (~32 km.) South of where you are standing. No joke! They really suggested this to me.

My usual way of crossing a bridge who's operating authority has such an attitude is to stand at entrance to the highway leading to the Bridge and try to hitch a ride. It usually works.

The Michigan DOT does have a pickup truck to transport you across this Bridge. Call 313 984-3131.

74.5 (119.9)   M 136 @ M 25   0.9 (1.4)
Continue traveling North on M 25.

75.4 (121.4)   Blue Water Bridges @ M 25   0.0 (0.0)
Hey! You're at the Southern end of Lake Huron.
Port Huron MI information in the *Port Huron to Harbor Beach* segment.
Sarnia ON information in the *Grand Bend to Sarnia* segment.

South to North	**Port Huron**	North to South
↓ Read mi. (km.)	**to Detroit**	mi. (km.) Read ↑

LAKE ERIE TO LAKE HURON
CANADA ROUTE

North to South ↓ Read mi. (km.)	Sarnia to Windsor	South to North Read mi. (km.) ↑
0.0 (0.0)	Front St. @ Exmouth St. Turn West on to Exmouth St. SARNIA:	103.2 (166.2)
0.1 (0.2)	Venetian Blvd. @ Exmouth St. Continue traveling West on Exmouth St. The Sarnia Visitors Ctr. is on Venetian Blvd.	103.1 (166.0)
0.2 (0.3)	Harbour Rd. @ Exmouth St. Turn South on Harbour Rd.	103.0 (165.8)
0.4 (0.6)	Waterfront Trail @ Harbour Rd. Travel South on the Trail.	102.8 (165.5)
1.1 (1.8)	Locheil St. @ Waterfront Trail Exit the Trail on to Locheil St.	102.1 (164.4)
1.2 (1.9)	Front St. @ Locheil St. Turn South on to Front St.	102.0 (164.2)
1.7 (2.7)	Johnston St. @ Front St. Turn East on to Johnston St.	101.5 (163.4)
1.8 (2.9)	Christina St. S. @ Johnston St. Turn South on to Christina St.	101.4 (163.3)
2.2 (3.5)	Confederation St. @ Christina St. Turn East on to Confederation St.	101.1 (162.8)
2.4 (3.9)	Vidal St./Brock St. @ Confederation St. Turn South on to Vidal St. Northbound cyclists will arrive at the intersection of Brock St. (1 way going N. for a block or two from a Y intersection with Vidal St.)	100.8 (162.3)
4.4 (7.1)	St. Clair Pkwy./Churchill Line @ Vidal St. Look for the entrance to the St. Clair Pkwy. Trail. Or begin bicycling on the roadway.	98.8 (159.1)

Sarnia to Chatham

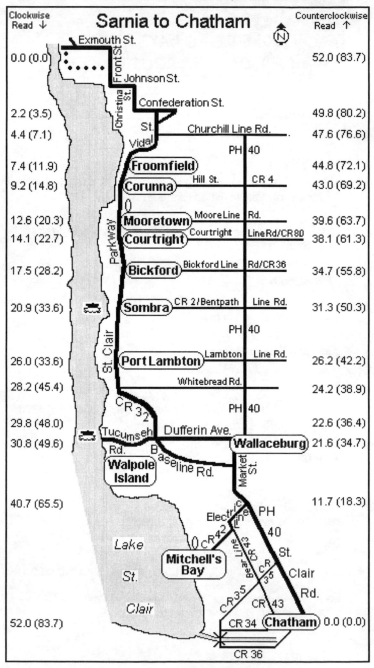

Clockwise Read ↓		Counterclockwise Read ↑

N

Exmouth St.

0.0 (0.0)   52.0 (83.7)

Front St.

Johnson St.

Christina St.

Confederation St.

2.2 (3.5)   49.8 (80.2)

St.

4.4 (7.1)   Churchill Line Rd.   47.6 (76.6)

Vidal   PH 40

7.4 (11.9)   **Froomfield**   44.8 (72.1)

9.2 (14.8)   **Corunna**   Hill St.   CR 4   43.0 (69.2)

12.6 (20.3)   **Mooretown**   Moore Line Rd.   39.6 (63.7)

Parkway

14.1 (22.7)   **Courtright**   Courtright   Line Rd./CR 80   38.1 (61.3)

17.5 (28.2)   **Bickford**   Bickford Line Rd./CR 36   34.7 (55.8)

20.9 (33.6)   **Sombra**   CR 2/Bentpath   Line Rd.   31.3 (50.3)

St. Clair   PH 40

26.0 (33.6)   **Port Lambton**   Lambton   Line Rd.   26.2 (42.2)

28.2 (45.4)   Whitebread Rd.   24.2 (38.9)

CR 32   PH 40

29.8 (48.0)   Dufferin Ave.   22.6 (36.4)

Tucumseh

30.8 (49.6)   **Wallaceburg**   21.6 (34.7)

Rd.   B

Walpole Island   Baseline Rd.   Market St.

40.7 (65.5)   11.7 (18.3)

Electric Line PH

Lake   CR 42   40

St.   **Mitchell's Bay**   Bear Line CR 43 St.

CR 35   Clair

CR 35   CR 43 Rd.

Clair

52.0 (83.7)   CR 34   **Chatham**   0.0 (0.0)

CR 36

9.2 (14.8)   Hill St./L 4 @ St. Clair Pkwy.   94.0 (151.3)
Continue traveling on the St. Clair Pkwy.

CORUNNA
Info.: St. Clair Pkwy. Comm., 242 St. Clair Pkwy., Corunna ON N0N 1G0, 519 862-2291. St. Clair Cons. Area, 519 245-3710.
Lodging: B&B: Mohawk, 413 Beresford St., 862-3840.

12.6 (20.3)   Moore Line @ St. Clair Pkwy.   90.6 (145.9)
Continue traveling on the St. Clair Pkwy.

MOORETOWN
Attraction: Moore Mus., 94 Moore Line, 867-2020; St. Clair River Trail, 1155 Emily St., Mooretown ON N0M 1M0, 867-3148, www.xcelco.on.ca/~stclair. AC: 519.
Lodging: B&B: Moore Lodge, 1509 Moore Line, 864-1880.
Camping: Mooretown, 1094 Emily St., 867-2951.

14.1 (22.7)   Courtright Line/L 80 @ Pkwy.   89.1 (143.5)
Continue traveling on the St. Clair Pkwy. COURTRIGHT

17.5 (28.2)   Bickford Line/L 36 @ Pkwy.   85.4 (137.5)
Continue traveling on the St. Clair Pkwy. Begin bicycling on the roadway. BICKFORD

20.9 (33.6)   Bentpath Line/ L 2@ Pkwy.   82.3 (132.5)
Continue traveling on the St. Clair Pkwy.

SOMBRA
Info.: Transportation: Bluewater Ferry, Sombra ON-Marine City MI, Dock, 888 638-4726.
Attraction: Sombra Township Mus., 3470 St. Clair Pkwy.
Lodging: B&B: Sombra, 160 Smith St., 892-3311.
Camping: Branton-Cundick Pk., CR 33 N., 892-3968; Cathcart Pk., St. Clair Pkwy, 892-3342.

26.0 (41.9)   Lambton Line @ St. Clair Pkwy.   77.2 (124.3)
Continue traveling on the St. Clair Pkwy.
PORT LAMBTON: **Lodging:** B&B: Rosie's, 3853 St. Clair Pkwy., 892-3581.

28.2 (45.4)   Whitebread Line   75.0 (120.8)
           @ St. Clair Pkwy./L 33
Southbound: The "official" Parkway ends, continue traveling South on the on L 33.
Northbound: Travel North on the St. Clair Pkwy.

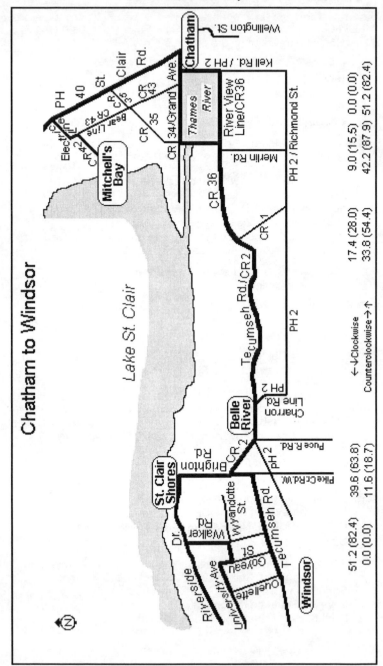

Chatham to Windsor

29.8 (48.0)   Baseline Rd./CK 33   73.5 (118.3)
               @ Payne Rd./CK 33
Continue traveling South on Baseline Rd./CK 33.

30.8 (49.6)   Dufferin Rd./CK 32   72.4 (116.6)
               @ Baseline Rd./CK 33
Turn East on to Dufferin Rd./CK 32.
Transportation: Turn West on to CR/32/Tucumseh Rd. to go to Walpole Island and the Ferry to Algonac MI via the Ferry. Traveling via this ferry to Detroit & Windsor will cut off ~97 km. (60 mi.) It is ~5 km. (3 mi.) from this intersection to the Ferry. This ferry has an irregular schedule. Make certain it is operating before traveling to the ferry dock.

WALPOLE ISLAND:
Services: Transportation: Algonac - Walpole Is. Ferry, Dock.
Lodging: Camping: Chemalogan, River Rd. S., 627-1558.

32.7 (52.6)   PH 40 Jct. Dufferin Rd./CR 32   70.5 (113.5)
Continue traveling East on PH 40.

35.1 (56.5)   McNaughton Ave./PH 40   68.1 (109.6)
               @ Dufferin Rd. PH 40
Turn South on to McNaughton Ave./PH 40.

WALLACEBURG
Attractions: Wallaceburg Mus., 505 King St., 627-8962; WISH Ctr. Af. Am Hist, 177 King St. E., 354-5248; Uncle Tom's Cabin Mus., 29251 Uncle Tom's Rd., Dresden, 683-2978.
Lodging: Motels

40.7 (65.5)   CK 42/Electric Line   62.5 (100.6)
               @ PH 40/St. Clair Rd.
Continue traveling on PH 40.
Turn West on to CK 42/Electric Line for Mitchell's Bay.

MITCHELL'S BAY
Lodging: B&B: Dity's at the Bay, 50 Main St., Mitchell's Bay, 519 354-5235; Parkside, RR#1, Dover Centre, (off PH 40 near Mitchells Bay), 352-4935. Camping: St. Clair Pkwy., Mitchell's Bay 354-8423.

A bit further South on PH 40 you can turn Southwest on to CK 35/St. Andrews Rd. and follow it through the countryside to the Thames River at CK 36/River View Rd. where you'll meet the main route to Windsor once again. CK 35/Andrews Rd. is about 11 km. (7 mi.) from this intersection.

52.0 (83.7)   Grand Ave. W./PH 2   51.2 (82.4)
                     @ St. Clair St./PH 40
Turn West on to Grand Ave. W./PH 2.

CHATHAM

Info.: Mun. of Chatham-Kent, 315 King St. W., Chatham, ON N7M 5K8, 800 561-6125/519 360-1998, AC: 519.
Attractions: Chatham-Kent Mus., 75 William St. N., 354-8338; Chatham Railroad Mus., McLean St., 352-3097; J & J Doll Mus., 10364 Fairview Line, 351-4389; Milner House, 75 William St. N., 354-8338.
Lodging: Jordan House, 7725 Eighth Line, 436-0839; Teresa's, 137 St.Clair St., 352-8982;

53.5 (86.1)   Grand Ave. W./PH 2/CK 34   49.7 (80.0)
                     @ Kell Rd./PH 2
Either continue traveling on Grand Ave. W./CK 34;
Or turn South on Kell Rd., cross the Thames River, and turn West on to River View Line/CK 36 immediately after crossing the River. The distance is about the same whether you travel North or South of the Thames River on CK 34 or CK 36.

61.0 (98.2)   CK 35/Jacob St.   42.2 (67.9)
                     @ CK 36/River View Line
                     CK 35/Jacob St.
                     @ CK 34/Grande River Rd./Grand St. W.
Continue traveling on CK 36/River View Line. If you took CK 35 or CK 34/Grande River Rd./Grand Ave. W. cross the River to the South bank.

61.6 (99.2)   CK 7/Merlin Rd.   41.6 (67.0)
                     @ CK 36/River View Rd./Tecumseh Line
Continue traveling on CK 36 which is now called Tecumseh Line.

69.4 (111.7)   E 2/Tecumseh Rd.   33.8 (54.4)
                     @ E 36/Tecumseh Line
Continue traveling on E 2/Tecumseh Rd. We've crossed a Municipal boundary and the road numbers and name change.

84.2 (135.6)   Notre Dame St. @ Tecumseh Rd.   19.0 (30.6)
Continue traveling on Notre Dame St. which once again becomes Tecumseh Rd. but this time PH 2 after you cross the Belle River. BELLE RIVER

87.8 (141.4)   Puce River Rd.   15.4 (24.8)
                    @ Tecumseh Rd./PH 2
        Turn North on to Puce River Rd.

88.0 (141.7)   Tecumseh Rd./E 2   15.2 (24.5)
                    @ Puce River Rd.
        Turn West on to Tecumseh Rd./E 2.

91.6 (147.5)   Brighton Rd./Tecumseh Rd.   11.6 (18.7)
                    @ Tecumseh Rd./E 2
        Turn North on to Brighton Rd.
        Or Turn South and then West following Tecumseh Rd.
        Tecumseh Rd./E 2 cuts diagonally through Windor and
        its suburbs, saving a few miles/kilometers. ST. CLAIR
        BEACH

91.9 (148.0)   Riverside Dr. @ Brighton Rd.   11.3 (18.2)
        Turn West on to Riverside Dr. As you go closer to the
        center of Windsor traffic increases.

101.0 (162.6)   Walker Rd. @ Riverside Dr.   2.2 (3.5)
        Turn on to Walker Rd. VIARail Station.

101.3 (163.1)   Wyandotte St. E. @ Walker Rd.   1.9 (3.1)
        Turn South (i. e., right) on to Wyandotte St. East.

102.8 (165.5)   Goyeau St. @ Wyandotte St. E.   0.4 (0.6)
        Turn West on to Goyeau St.
        You could continue 2 more blocks to Ouelette St./PH 3B
        but its a very busy fast moving road. You're at the
        Windsor-Detroit Tunnel entrance. You want to be 2
        blocks West at the bus terminal.

103.1 (166.0)   University Ave. W. @ Goyeau St.   0.1 (0.2)
        Turn South on to University Ave. W.

103.2 (166.2)   Freedom Way @ University Ave. W.   0.0 (0.0)
        Windsor Transit Bus Terminal.

Clockwise	**Windsor**	Counterclockwise
↓ Read mi. (km.)	**to Sarnia**	Read mi. (km.) ↑

Montpelier OH to Toledo OH

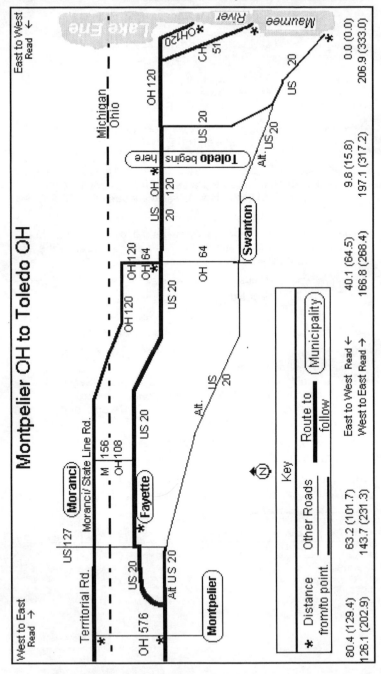

LAKE ERIE TO LAKE MICHIGAN

East to West Read down ↓	**Toledo to** **New Buffalo**	West to East Read up ↑

0.0 (0.0)   Maumee River   206.9 (333.0)
                       @ OH 51 or OH120
Travel West on either OH 51, OH 120 or US 20 depending
on where you cross the River.
Toledo info. is in the Pt. Clinton to Toledo segment.

9.8 (15.8)   Toledo City border   197.1 (317.2)
                        @ OH120/US20
OH 120 jct. with US 20 just a bit to the east of this point.
OH 120 maintains its number designation as it traverses
Indiana and Michigan.
SWANTON: **Info.:** Swanton Area CofC, 100 Broadway,
Swanton OH 43558, 419 826-1941. Swanton lodging in-
formation is available from the Toledo CVB.

40.1 (64.5)   OH 64/OH 120 @ US 20   166.8 (268.4)
Continue traveling West on US 20.
Alternatively, turn North on OH 64/OH 120 and follow OH
120 West. OH 120 is less heavily trafficked than US 20.

63.2 (101.7)   US 127 @ US 20   143.7 (231.3)
Continue traveling West on US 20. After crossing the
Ohio-Michigan border OH 120 becomes Moranci/State
Line Rd. and further West after Moranci MI becomes M
120/Territorial Rd.
FAYETTE OH: **Info.:** Fayette County CofC, 101 East St.,
Washington OH 43160, 740 335-0761.
Lodging: Motels. B&Bs: Red Brick Inn 206 W. Main St.,
Fayette OH 43521, 419 237-2276. Camping: Harrison
Lake St. Pk.

80.4 (129.4)   OH 576 @ US 20   126.1 (202.9)
Travel West on US 20.
MONTPELIER OH: Montpelier OH CofC, 410 W. Main St.,
Montpelier OH 43543, 419 485-4416.

98.9 (159.2)   IN 827 @ US 20   108.0 (173.8)
Continue traveling West on US 20.
ANGOLA: **Info.:** AngolaCofC, 1205 N. Wayne St., Angola
IN 46703, 219 665-3512. FREMONT: **Info.:** Fremont
CofC, PO Box 462, Fremont IN 46737, 219 495-9010.

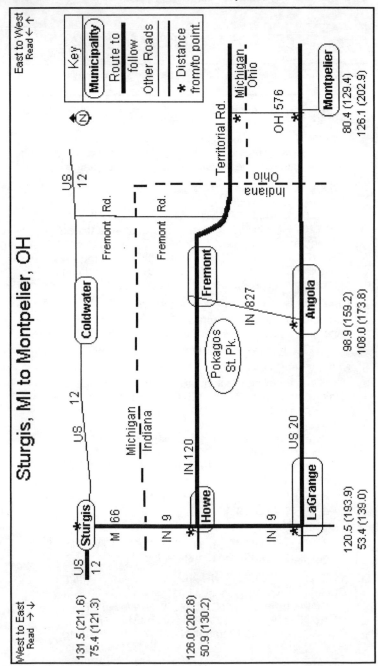

Sturgis, MI to Montpelier, OH

120.5 (193.9)   IN 9 @ US 20   86.4 (139.0)
Turn North on to IN 9. LaGrange IN

LAGRANGE

Info.: Shipshewana / LaGrange County CVB, 440½ S. Van Buren St., Shipshewana IN 46565, 260 768-4008. LaGrange CofC, 512 N. Detroit St., LaGrange IN 46761, 260 463-2443. ZC: 46761. AC: 260.

Attraction: LaGrange is in Amish country watch for horse carriages & gawking auto tourists.

Lodging: Motels. B&Bs: M&M, 215 N. Detroit St., La-Grange IN, 463-2961

Holmestead, 4330 W. 200 S., La Grange IN, 463-7544.

126.0 (202.8)   IN 9   80.9 (130.2)
            @ IN 120 (OH 120/MI 120 Territorial Rd.)
Continue North on IN 9.

HOWE: **Lodging:** Motels. B&B: Pleasant Vale Farm, 4810 E. 500 N., 260 562-2965. Camping: Twin Mills Camping Resort, 1675 W. IN 120, Howe IN, 260 562-3212.

131.5 (211.6)   US 12 @ IN 9/M 66   75.4 (121.3)
Turn West on to US 12. You've crossed into Michigan and IN 9 suddenly became MI 66!

STURGIS

Info.: River Country Tourism, PO Box 187, Sturgis MI 49091, 800 447-2821. AC: 269. ZC: 49091.

Serv.: Kickstand Schwin Cyclery, 1240 E. Chicago, Sturgis MI 49091, 269 651-5088. Bike loop map available.

Lodging: Motels. B&Bs: Christmere, 110 Pleasant St., 269 651-8303.

Camping: Green Valley Cpgd., 25499 W. Fawn River Rd., 651-8760.

143.5 (230.9)   Redfield Rd./Bertland Rd.   63.4 (102.0)
            @ US 12
Continue traveling on US 12. Alternatively use Redfield Rd./Bertland Rd. for about 33 mi (53 km.) to York Red Blvd. At York Red Blvd. turn North to retlurn to US 12.

164.5 (264.7)   M 82 @ US 12   42.4 (68.2)
Continue traveling on US 12. Lake Erie bound cyclists can turn South on M 82 and then turn East on Bertland/ Redfield Rd. to rejoin US 12 in about 12 mi.

EDWARDSBURG: Edwardsburg CofC, PO Box 575, Edwardsburg MI 49112, 616 663-2023.

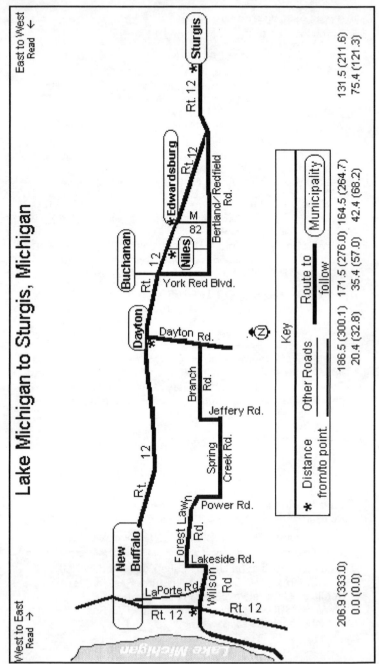

Lake Michigan to Sturgis, Michigan

171.5 (276.0)   Niles Rd. @ US 12   35.4 (57.0)
Continue traveling on US 12. Turn off for Niles MI.

BUCHANAN & NILES

Info.: Four Flags Area Council on Tourism, 321 E. Main St., Niles MI 49120, 269 684-7444. Buchanan CofC, 119 Main St., Buchanan MI 49107, 269 695-3291. ZC: Niles 49120, Buchanan: 49107. AC: 269.
Attraction: US 12 Heritage Trail, 467-5522.
Lodging: Motels: Lodging: Motels. Camping: Fuller's Clear Lake Cpgd., 1622 East Clear Lake Road, Buchanan, 695-3785; Nub Lake Cpgd., 1701 Pucker St. Dr., 683-0670; Spaulding Lake Cpgd., 2305 Bell Rd., Niles, 684-1393.

186.5 (300.1)   Dayton Rd. @ US 12   20.4 (32.8)
Continue traveling West on US 12. Dayton MI

206.9 (333.0)   Lake Michigan @ US 12   0.0 (0.0)
Hey, you're here! go North on US 23 or South on US 12.

NEW BUFFALO

Info.: Harbor Country CVB, 530 S. Whittaker St., Ste. F, New Buffalo MI 49117. AC: 269.
Lodging: Motels. B&Bs: Lodging: Motels. B&Bs: Sans Souci, 19265 S. Lakeside Rd., 756-3141; Tall Oaks Inn, 19400 Ravine Rd., 469-0097. Camping: Bob-A-Ron Cpgd. & Resort, 7650 Warren Woods Rd., Three Oaks MI 49128, 469-3894; Warren Dunes St. Pk., 12032 Red Arrow Hwy., Sawyer MI 49125, 426-4013.

East to West	**New Buffalo to**	West to East
Read down ↓	**Toledo**	Read up ↑

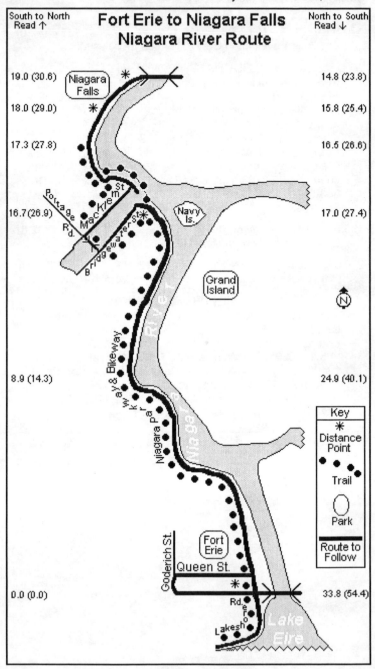

Fort Erie to Niagara Falls
Niagara River Route

South to North
Read ↑

North to South
Read ↓

19.0 (30.6) Niagara Falls 14.8 (23.8)

18.0 (29.0) 15.8 (25.4)

17.3 (27.8) 16.5 (26.6)

Portage Rd.

Macklem St.

16.7 (26.9) 17.0 (27.4)

Bridgewater St.

Navy Is.

Grand Island

8.9 (14.3) 24.9 (40.1)

Niagara parkway & Bikeway

Niagara River

Key

✳ Distance Point

● Trail

◯ Park

━ Route to Follow

Goderich St.

Fort Erie

Queen St.

0.0 (0.0) 33.8 (54.4)

Rd.

Lakesh

Lake Eire

LAKE ERIE TO LAKE ONTARIO
CANADA NIAGARA RIVER ROUTE:

South to North Read down ↓	Fort Erie to Niagara-On-The-Lake	North to South Read up ↑
00.0 (0.0)	Canadian Customs @ Peace Bridge	33.8 (54.4)

Exit the Bridge area by bearing on to Queen St. via the tourist information building. FORT ERIE.

| 0.1 (0.2) | Queen St. @ Goderich St. | 33.7 (54.2) |

Turn West on to Queen St.

| 0.3 (0.5) | Niagara Pkwy. @ Queen St. | 33.5 (53.9) |

Turn North on to the Niagara Parkway Trail which sometimes is and sometimes is not actually an off road bicycle trail. You are at the Niagara River looking at Park.

| 14.0 (22.5) | Battle of Chippewa Battlefield
@ Niagara Pkwy. | 19.8 (31.9) |

Continue traveling on the Parkway or look for the off road trail on the River side of Niagara Parkway.

| 15.3 (24.6) | Welland River Bridge
@ Niagara Pkwy Trail | 18.5 (29.8) |

Cross the roadway and follow the Trail to the bike/pedestrian Bridge over the Welland River. Alternative road route: Follow Niagara Parkway around the shore line of the Welland River to where it becomes Bridgewater St. At Willoughby Dr. cross the River on the roadway Bridge.

| 15.5 (24.9) | Kings Bridge Pk.
@ Trail Welland River | 18.2 (29.3) |

Cross the River using the bike/pedestrian Trail Bridge over the Welland River. Alternative road route: South bound cyclists can exit the Trail & Kings Bridge Park on to Niagara Parkway @ MacKlem St. Follow MacKlem St. to the roadway bridge at Portage St. and cross the River on to Willoughby Dr.

| 16.7 (26.9) | Control Dam Bike-Ped Bridge
@ Trail | 17.0 (27.4) |

Use the Bike-Ped Bridge to cross the water!

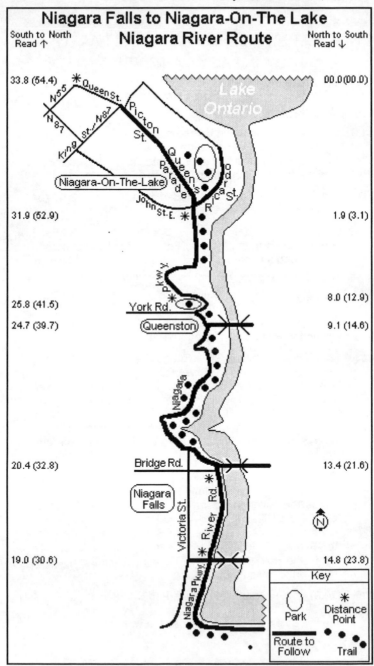

Niagara Falls to Niagara-On-The Lake
Niagara River Route

South to North
Read ↑

North to South
Read ↓

33.8 (54.4)   00.0 (00.0)

Lake Ontario

Queen St.
N 55
N 87
Picton St.
King St. / N 87
Queens
Parade
Niagara-On-The-Lake
Ricardo St.
John St. E.

31.9 (52.9)   1.9 (3.1)

Pkwy

York Rd.
25.8 (41.5)   8.0 (12.9)

Queenston
24.7 (39.7)   9.1 (14.6)

Niagara

Bridge Rd.
20.4 (32.8)   13.4 (21.6)

Niagara Falls

Victoria St.
River Rd.

N

19.0 (30.6)   14.8 (23.8)

Niagara Pkwy

Key

○ Park   ✳ Distance Point

●●● Route to Follow   ●●● Trail

17.3 (27.8)   Power House @ Trail   16.5 (26.6)
Once again you're cycling near the Niagara Parkway
roadway. The Greenhouses are across the road!

18.0 (29.0)   Table Top Rock Tourism Ctr.   15.8 (25.4)
                     @ Niagara Pkwy./River Rd./Trail
This is the beginning of the crowded tourist area. No bicycle riding on the walkway near the Falls. Ride on the
roadway. Use extreme care. Drivers are not paying atten-
tion to the roadway. They are craning their necks to look
at the Falls. The roadway is heavily trafficked from this
point to the Whirlpool Bridge area. There is no bike path.
This is a high bicycle theft area. Double lock your bicycle.
Watch your panniers. If you do participate in an attraction
(e. g., the Table Rock Scenic Tunnels or Maid of the Mist
Boat, etc.) then make certain your bicycle is in a position
which can be watched by someone. Personally, I leave
my pannier laden bike at my lodging and use the *People
Mover* or my feet to visit the attractions.
Niagara Parkway becomes River Road at this point.

NIAGARA FALLS
Info.: Niagara Falls Tourism, 5515 Stanley Ave., 356-6061; Niagara Parks Comm., Box 150, 356-2241. AC 905. PC: Various.
Services: All
Attractions: Many, pick up a brochure at *Table Rock*.
Lodging: Motels and hotels at all price ranges. Backpacker & HI
hostels. Camping (most campgrounds are RV based camping:
Campark Resorts Best Holiday Trav-L-Pk., 9387 Lundy's Ln. (Hwy
20), 358-3873; King Waldorf's Tent & Trailer Pk., Stanley Ave.,
295-8191; Niagara Falls KOA, 8625 Lundy's Ln., 356-2267; Niag-
ara Glen-view, 3950 Victoria Ave., 358-8689; Orchard Grove
TTPk., 8123 Lundy's Ln., 358-9883; Riverside Pk. Cpgd., Niagara
R. Pkwy., 382-2204; Scott's TT Pk., Lundy's Ln. W. 356-6988;
Yogi Bear's Jellystone Pk., 8676 Oakwood Dr., 354-1432; Shala-
mar Lake, Niagara R. Pkwy & Line Rd. 8, 262-4895, Queenston.

19.0 (30.6)   Rainbow Bridge @ River Rd.   14.8 (23.8)
Continue traveling on Niagara Parkway. Casino area.
The Rainbow Bridge has a walkway.

20.4 (32.8)   Whirlpool Bridge/Bridge St.   13.4 (21.6)
                     @ River Rd.
Continue traveling on Niagara Pkwy.
Traveling West on Bridge St. for .2 mi. (.3 km.) brings
you to both the bus station and the VIARail station.

You may not be able to transport an unboxed or even a boxed bike on the train. The bus station has those wonderful bike bags for transporting your bike on the bus and possibly the train (ask at the train station).

21.4 (34.4)   Victoria St. @ River Rd.   12.4 (20.0)
                 @ Niagara Pkwy. Trail
The off road Trail begins again here. Look on the River side of the Pkwy. River Rd. becomes Niagara Pkwy.

22.6 (36.4)   Wintergreen Flat @ Pkwy. Trail   11.1 (17.9)
The off road Trail crosses the Pkwy. and continues northward on the West (non-River) side of the Pkwy.

23.7 (38.1)   Butterfly Conservatory   10.1 (16.3)
                 @ Pkwy./Trail
Trail crosses the Pkwy. and continues northward on the River side of the roadway.

24.7 (39.7)   Queenston-Lewiston Bridge   9.1 (14.6)
                 @ Pkwy./Trail
Continue on your way. If you are crossing the Niagara River to the USA, look for the entrance to the Bridge just before the overhead roadway (as you are traveling northward.) Entering the Bridge here will bring you at the Customs station & the walkway. However bicycles are allowed to cross this Bridge using the roadway.

25.2 (40.6)   Under Pkwy. underpass @ Trail   8.6 (13.8)
Continue following the Trail. It goes under the Niagara Pkwy. and into Locust Grove Pk. and Brock's Memorial National Hist. Monument. It circles around Brock's Monument and exits on to the Niagara Parkway.

25.8 (41.5)   Niagara Pkwy./York Rd./N 81   8.0 (12.9)
                 @ Trail in Brock's Mem. NHS
The Trail's northern exit from Brock's Mem. Nat'l. HIst. Site places you at York Rd./St./N 81 and the Parkway. You're cycling on the western edge of Queenston on the Niagara Parkway roadway. N 81/York Rd. traverses the Niagara Peninsula all the way to Hamilton. "'Round Lake Ontario: A Bicyclist's Tour Guide" uses this road, N 81, as the primary route to Hamilton. It is also the "Wine Tour" route. There are many wineries along N 81.

27.0 (43.5)   Weir Art Mus. @ Parkway   6.8 (10.9)
Once again there is an off road trail at this point. It is the General Brock Trail and hugs the River's shore line.

31.9 (51.3)   Queen's Parade @ Niagara Pkwy   1.9 (3.1)
Trail @ Ricardo St. Niagara Pkwy. @ Ricardo St./John
St. Continue on the Trail or descend into Niagara-on-the-
Lake via Queen's Parade (the entry road into Niagara-on-
the-Lake.)

32.4 (52.1)   Ricardo St. @ Trail   1.4 (2.3)
Ft. George NHPk @ Trail Follow the trail through Fort
George National Historic Site. You will emerge from the
Hist. Site on to Queen's Parade.

32.9 (52.9)   Queens Parade @ Trail   0.9 (1.4)
                     Queens Parade @ Ft. George
Turn North on to Queen's Parade. South bound cyclists
should definitely enter the Trail and ride along the edge
of Ft. George.

33.2 (53.4)   Picton St. @ Queen's Parade   0.6 (1.0)
Continue traveling straight on Picton St. In 1 block Picton
St. becomes Queen St. South bound cyclists should

33.4 (53.8)   Picton St. @ King St./N 87   0.4 (0.6)
Picton St. @ Queen St. Continue traveling straight on to
Queen St. Turn South on to King St./ N 87 which becomes Mary St. and then Lake Shore Rd./N 87. Lake
Shore Rd. / N 87 closely follows the Lake Ontario shore
line until well past St. Catharines. *'Round Lake Ontario...*
uses N 87 as a primary route around Lake Ontario.

33.8 (54.4)   Mississauga St. / N 55   0.0 (0.0)
                     @ Queen St.
Continue traveling Northwest to see Lake Ontario at the
end of Queen St. Fort Mississauga Nat'l. Hist. Site gives
you a good view of the intersection of the Niagara River
and Lake Ontario. Across the River from Fort Mississauga is Old Fort Niagara St. Hist. Pk. in New York
State. Mississauga St./N 55 becomes Niagara Stone Rd.
and will take you to the Welland Canal in St. Catharines.

South to North	**Niagara-On-The-Lake**	North to South
Read down ↓	**to Fort Erie**	Read up ↑

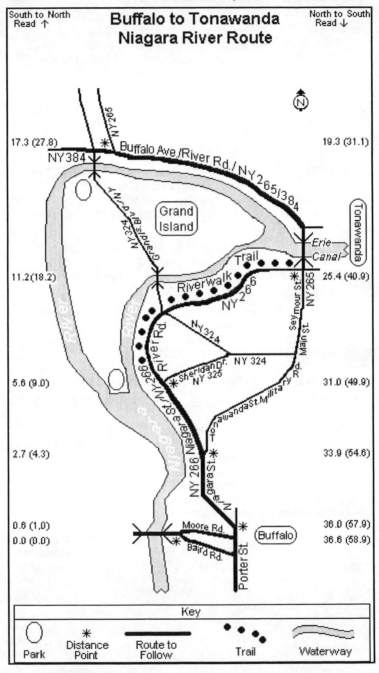

South to North
Read ↑

Buffalo to Tonawanda
Niagara River Route

North to South
Read ↓

17.3 (27.8)

NY 384

Buffalo Ave./River Rd./NY 265/384

19.3 (31.1)

Grand Island

Tonawanda

Erie Canal

Trail

Riverwalk

11.2 (18.2)

NY 265

25.4 (40.9)

Seymour St.

NY 324

Main St.

Sheridan Dr.
NY 325

NY 324

5.6 (9.0)

River Rd.

31.0 (49.9)

Tonawanda St. Military Rd.

2.7 (4.3)

NY 266 Niagara St.

Niagara St.

33.9 (54.6)

0.6 (1,0)

Moore Rd.

Buffalo

36.0 (57.9)

0.0 (0.0)

Baird Rd.

Porter St.

36.6 (58.9)

Key

| Park | Distance Point | Route to Follow | Trail | Waterway |

LAKE ERIE TO LAKE ONTARIO
USA NIAGARA RIVER ROUTE

South to North Read down ↓	**Buffalo to** **Youngstown**	North to South Read up ↑

00 (0.0)   USA Customs @ Peace Bridge   36.6 (58.9)
After going through Customs & Immigration bicycle
straight through Perry Mon. Park. to Porter St.

0.3 (0.5)   Porter St. @ Baird Dr./Moore Dr.   36.3 (58.4)
Turn North (left) on to Porter St. from Baird Dr. Cyclists
going to the Bridge will turn West on to Moore Dr.

0.6 (1.0)   Niagara St./NY 266 @ Porter St.   36.0 (57.9)
Turn West on to Niagara St./NY 266.

1.3 (2.1)   Niagara River   35.3 (56.8)
                    @ Niagara St./NY 266
Continue following Niagara St. North. Just an indication
that you are now cycling near the River. You may be able
to locate an off-road bicycle trail near the River. It is there
for your use!

2.7 (4.3)   Tonawanda St./NY 265   33.9 (54.6)
                    @ Niagara St./NY 266
Bear Northwest and continue traveling on Niagara St./NY
266. If you prefer cycling through residential areas then
use Tonawanda St./NY 265 to go North. The two roads
intersect 8.3 mi. (13.4 km.) further north in Tonawanda at
the Erie Canal.

5.6 (9.0)   Sheridan Dr./NY 325   31.0 (49.9)
                    @ River Rd./NY 266
Niagara St. has changed its name to "River Rd./NY 266."
Continue following NY 266.
Or look for the off-road Riverwalk Trail and use it.

7.8 (12.6)   Grand Island Blvd./324 @ River Rd./NY 266
                    28.8 (46.3)
Onwards along the River on either the Riverwalk Trail or
River Rd./NY 266. There is a pedestrian walkway on the
South Interstate 190 Grand Island Bridge.

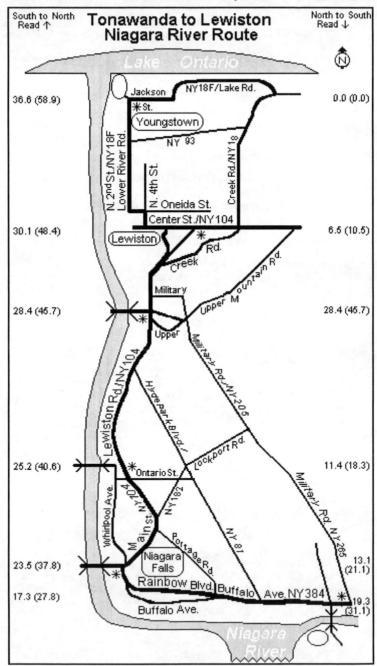

Tonawanda to Lewiston
Niagara River Route

South to North Read ↑

North to South Read ↓

Lake Ontario

NY18F/Lake Rd.

Jackson St.

Youngstown

NY 93

36.6 (58.9)

0.0 (0.0)

N. 2nd St./NY18F Lower River Rd.

Creek Rd./NY 18

N. 4th St.

N. Oneida St.

Center St./NY 104

Lewiston

30.1 (48.4)

6.5 (10.5)

Creek Rd.

Upper Mountain Rd.

Military

28.4 (45.7)

28.4 (45.7)

Upper

Lewiston Rd./NY 104

Hyde Park Blvd./

Military Rd./NY 205

Lockport Rd.

Ontario St.

25.2 (40.6)

11.4 (18.3)

Whirlpool Ave.

NY 104

NY 182

NY 81

Military Rd./NY 265

Main St.

Portage Rd.

Niagara Falls

Rainbow Blvd.

Buffalo Ave. NY 384

23.5 (37.8)

13.1 (21.1)

17.3 (27.8)

Buffalo Ave.

19.3 (31.1)

Niagara River

9.4 (15.1)   Two Mile Creek Rd./N 524   27.2 (43.8)
                    @ Riverwalk Trail
                    @ River Rd./Niagara St./NY 266
If you are cycling on River Rd. go on to the Trail, it is a
delightful ride along the shore. River Rd. changes its
name, once again, to Niagara St./NY 266 as you enter
the Town of Tonawanda.

11.0 (17.7)   Tonawanda Creek/Erie Canal   25.6 (41.2)
                    @ Riverwalk Trail Niagara St./NY 266
                    @ Seymour St./NY 265
Follow the Trail as it makes an eastward turn. You are
now a the western terminus of the Erie Canal. The letter-
ing in the sign across the Canal is large enough to show
up in a picture! NY 266 ends at this point. No, you don't
drop off the face of the earth because the road ends!

11.2 (18.0)   Seymour St./NY 265 Bridge   25.4 (40.9)
                    @ Riverwalk Trail
Use the cloverleaf exit from the Trail to go to the roadway
on the NY 265/Seymour St./River Rd. Bridge. Since the
street names continually change follow the numbered
road signs when they are provided. There is a nice park
along the Canal.

11.3 (18.2)   River Rd./NY 265   25.3 (40.7)
                    @ Seymour St./NY 265 Bridge
Travel North on River Rd./NY 265. Yes, its the same
street as Seymour St. but you are now in North Tonawanda and the street name has changed. South bound
cyclists should use the cloverleaf exit from the NY 265
Bridge leading to the Riverwalk Trail.

11.7 (18.8)   Main St./NY 384   24.9 (40.1)
                    @ River Rd./NY 265
Continue traveling on River Rd./NY 265 & NY 384.

16.3 (26.2)   Williams Pkwy   20.3 (32.7)
                    @ River Rd./NY265 & NY 384
River Rd./NY 265-384 changes its name to Buffalo Ave./
NY 265-384. You are now traveling due West on NY 265-
384 even though the signs say North (or South). The geography of the River makes this direction change necessary.

17.3 (27.8)   S. Military Rd./NY 265   19.3 (31.1)
                   @ Buffalo Ave./NY 384
Continue following Buffalo Ave./NY 384 to go to the Rainbow Bridge and the "Falls." NY 265 turns North here and
cuts diagonally across the City of Niagara Falls to the
Queenston-Lewiston Canada-USA Bridge.

19.3 (31.1)   North Grand Is. Bridge   17.3 (27.8)
                   @ Buffalo Ave./NY 384
Pedestrian walkway?

20.9 (33.6)   Hyde Park Blvd./NY 81   15.7 (25.3)
                   @ Buffalo Ave./NY 384
Continue traveling on Buffalo Ave./NY 384. Hyde Park
Blvd. is the direct way to the northern Niagara Falls sub-
urbs by passing the "Falls."

22.5 (36.2)   Rainbow Blvd./NY 384   14.1 (22.7)
                   @ Buffalo Ave.
Either street will take you to the "Falls" and the Rainbow
Bridge. Rainbow Blvd./NY 384 is a bit more heavily traf-
ficked than Buffalo Ave.

23.2 (37.3)   1st St. @ Rainbow Blvd./NY 384   13.4 (21.6)
                   @ Buffalo Ave. @ Prospect St.
Continue traveling to the Rainbow Bridge using NY 384/
Rainbow Blvd. or Buffalo Ave. Turn South on to 1st St. to
go to Goat Island and the Niagara Reservation St. Pk.
Buffalo Ave. changes its name to Prospect St. at this
point. Don't ask me why, its a really stupid street name
change. If you are planning to go to Canada or continue
North to Lake Ontario then you must turn North on to 1st
St. and go 1 block then turn West on to Rainbow Blvd.

23.5 (37.8)   Rainbow Bridge entrance   13.1 (21.1)
                   @ Rainbow Blvd./NY 384
                   @ Niagara St.
                   @ Main St./NY 104
Wow! What an intersection! North bound cyclists, going
to Lake Ontario or the Queenston-Lewiston Bridge use
Main St./NY 104. You can not bicycle on the Robert
Moses Parkway. South bound cyclists going to Buffalo
use Rainbow Blvd./NY 384. Canada bound cyclists turn
West into the Bridge area using the walkway on the
South side of the Bridge.

23.8 (38.3)   2nd St./Whirlpool St.   12.8 (20.6)
                     @ Main St./NY 104
Continue traveling North on Main St./NY 104. 2nd St./
Whirlpool St. goes along the River but there is really
nothing to see. It's a rutted street and only leads to the
Whirlpool Bridge entrance.

24.7 (39.7)   Portage St. @ Main St./NY 104   11.9 (19.2)
Bear Northwest and continue following Main St./NY 104.
South bound cyclists bear Southwest and continue to
follow Main St./NY 104.

24.8 (39.9)   Lockport Rd. @ Main St./NY 104   11.8 (19.0)
Continue following Main St./NY 104. Lockport Rd./NY
182 goes to Lockport and the Erie Canal. A 100 mi. (160
km.) off-road trail along the Canal begins at Lockport and
goes eastward.

25.2 (40.6)   Ontario St.   11.4 (18.3)
                     @ Main St.-Lewiston Rd./NY 104
Continue to follow the NY 104 signs. Main St. changes its
name to Lewiston Rd. as it goes northward. Turning
West, towards the River, on to Ontario St. will bring you
to the Whirlpool Bridge to Canada.

27.3 (43.9)   Hyde Park Blvd./NY 81   9.3 (15.0)
                     @ Lewiston Rd./NY 104
Continue traveling on Lewiston Rd./NY 104. Hyde Park
Blvd. cuts diagonally across the western edge of Niagara
Falls by passing the "Falls."

27.7 (44.6)   NY Power Auth.   8.9 (14.3)
                     @ Lewiston Rd./NY 104
Continue onwards or stop for a look at the power plant.
Good view of the River from the Visitors' Center.

28.4 (45.7)   Upper Mountain Rd.   8.2 (13.2)
                     @ Lewiston Rd./NY 104
Continue traveling on Lewiston Rd./NY 104 to go to Lake
Ontario. Turn East on to Upper Mountain Rd. to go to the
Lewiston-Queenston Bridge to Canada. The entrance to
the Bridge area is .5 mi. (.8 km.) from this intersection.
There is a narrow walkway on the Bridge or you may be
allowed to use the roadway if there is little motor traffic.

From Customs to Customs station the Bridge is ~1 mi. (1.6 km.) There used to be a bike-ped entrance leading directly to the walkway but it is now closed for security reasons. Note: Folks exiting the Queenston-Lewiston Bridge on to the USA side should exit on to Upper Mountain Rd. and then on to Lewiston Rd./NY 104. It is a very steep descent into Lewiston. Check your brakes.

29.0 (46.7)   Military Trail   7.6 (12.2)
                   @ Lewiston Rd./NY 104
Continue traveling on Lewiston Rd./NY 104. Cyclists reaching this point after the long steep ascent from Lewiston can turn here for the Bridge. I always miss this road and end up using Upper Mountain Rd. to go to the Bridge. It is ~1 mi. (1.6 km.) to the Bridge entrance.

30.1 (48.4)   Center St./NY 104   6.5 (10.5)
                   @ Lewiston Rd./NY 104
                   Center St./NY 18F @ Lewiston Rd./NY 104
                   Creek Rd./NY 18 @ Center St. NY104
At the bottom of the descent on NY 104/Lewiston Rd. from the Bridge you'll be on Center St. in Lewiston. This is NY 104 jct. NY 18F. Turn West on to NY 18 F/Center St. If by some chance you bared East on to Creek Rd. as you rapidly descended from the Bridge then turn West on to Center St./NY 18F. Creek St. is NY 18 and it does go to Lake Ontario but we're going to use 18F for its scenic beauty.

30.8 (49.6)   N. 4th St./NY 18F   5.8 (9.3)
                   @ Center St./NY 18F
Turn North on to N. 4th St./NY 18F.

31.0 (49.9)   Oneida St./NY 18F   5.6 (9.0)
                   @ N. 4th St./NY 18F
Turn West on to Oneida St./NY 18F.

31.2 (50.2)   N. 2nd St./NY 18F   5.4 (8.7)
                   @ Oneida St./NY 18F
Turn North on to N. 2nd St./NY 18F. N. 2nd St. changes its name to Lower River Rd. and then to Main St. as it goes north. It is NY 18F no matter what name it is called.

36.3 (58.4)   Main St./NY 18F.   0.3 (0.5)
                   @Youngstown-Lockport Rd./NY 93
Continue traveling on Main St./NY 18F. NY 93/ Youngstown-Lockport Rd. goes to Lockport and the Erie Canal.

36.6 (58.9)   Main St./NY 18F   0.0 (0.0)
                     @ Entrance to Fort Niagara St. Pk.
    It is ~1.5 mi. (2.4 km.) to Old Ft. Niagara and the Lake
    Ontario shore in the Park.
    Pop a wheelie and do a 180! You can either return from
    whence you came or travel counterclockwise around
    Lake Ontario from this point.
    If you are traveling East along Lake Ontario then do not
    enter the Park. Follow the 18Fsigns on to Jackson St.
    and then Lake Rd. Four Mile Creek St. Pk. is ~4.5 mi.
    (7.2 km.) from Ft. Niagara St. Pk.

South to North	**Youngstown**	North to South
Read down ↓	**to Buffalo**	Read up ↑

COMMENTS

I appreciate your comments. Please feel free to add comments.

Dates you toured _____.

Which chapters or information did you find most useful in:

　　　'Round Lake Erie: A Bicyclist's Tour Guide, 2nd Ed.
- ○ Tour Preparation
- ○ The Route
- ○ Distance Information
- ○ Lodging Information
- ○ Municipal Information
- ○ Other: _____

Lodging Recommendations

Attractions Recommendations

Restaurant/Bakery/Grocery Recommendations

Route Recommendations

Other Comments:

Your Name: _____

Your Address: _____

City, State/Prov., Zip/PC: _____

E-mail: _____

The name of a friend who might be interested in receiving our brochure:

Name: _____

Address: _____

City, State/Prov., Zip/PC: _____

E-mail: _____

We do not sell or rent our mailing list.

Please return this Comment Form to:
Cyclotour Guide Books, PO Box 10585, Rochester, NY 14610

Thanks,

Harvey

SURVEY FORM

One of the most significant problems facing bicycling advocates is the lack of data on cyclotourism and cyclotourists. It is almost impossible to make a case for improving roadway and general bicycle touring conditions unless cycling advocates have data on bicycle tourists.

This Survey is anonymous. You do not have to provide your name, etc. and I will not compare this Form to the *Comment Form*. That's why there are two separate forms.

I have tried to make this Survey Form easy for you to complete. Check the boxes or fill in the spaces, almost all of which are on the right side of the page. Sorry lefties!

'Round Lake Erie: A Bicyclist's Tour Guide, 2nd Ed.
I'll use the data when I lecture and write articles on bicycle touring.

How many people were in your touring party? _____

Demographic data of cyclotourists

Your age? _____ Sex? _____
Spouse's age? _____ Sex? _____
Child's age? _____ Sex? _____
Child's age? _____ Sex? _____
Friend's age? _____ Sex? _____
Friend's age? _____ Sex?_____
Friend's age? _____ Sex? _____

Your per annum income range:

O US $ O CAN $ O EURO €   O Other _____

Teenager on allowance?   O
College Student?   O
Below US$20,000   O
US $20,001 - $30,000   O
US $30,001 - $40,000   O
US $40,001 - $50,000   O
US $50,001 +   O

Enough of this demographic stuff but It is important for presenting a case for better bicycling conditions.

What was the total distance you toured? _____ mi. or km.
The average daily distance you traveled? _____ mi. or km.
Did you tour in segments? _____ How many? ____

Average amount of money expended each day, per person?
In ○ US $ ○ CAN $ ○ EURO ∈   ○ Other _____

Less than US$10.00	○
US $10.01 - 15.00	○
US $15.01 - 25.00	○
US $25.01 - 35.00	○
US $35.01 - 45.00	○
US $45.01 - 55.00	○
US $55.01 - 65.00	○
US $65.01 - 75.00	○
US $75.01 - 85.00	○
Over US $85.01	○

Average amount of money expended each day for these items:
In ○ US $ ○ CAN $ ○ EURO ∈   ○ Other _____

Amount	Lodging	Food, Incl.	Attractions	Misc.
Less than $5.00				
$5.01 - 10.00				
$10.01 - 20.00				
$20.01 - 25.00				
$25.01 - 30.00				
$30.01 +				

General description.of how you cyclotoured:

Loaded touring?	○
Camping & mainly eating in restaurants?	○
Sagwagon camping?	○
○ B&Bs ○ Motels & preparing own meals?	○
○ B&Bs ○ Motels & eating in restaurants?	○
Other: _____	○

Please return this form to: Cyclotour Guide Books, PO Box, 10585, Rochester, NY 14610. Thanks, Harvey.

EQUIPMENT LISTS

✓ Clothing
- ○ Cycling Short
- ○ Cycling Shorts
- ○ Cycling Shorts
- ○ Cycling Gloves
- ○ Off Cycling Shorts
- ○ Tee Shirts
- ○ Tee Shirts
- ○ Socks #_____
- ○ Short Socks #_____
- ○ Underwear
- ○ Jacket
- ○ Sweater/Fleece top
- ○ Dress pants
- ○ Long (thermal) Tights
- ○ Jeans
- ○ Rain Gear
- ○ Shoes
  - ○ Cycling
  - ○ Off-cycling
- ○ Dress
- ○ Blouse #_____
- ○ Shirt #_____
- ○ Wicking base layer
- ○ Bathing Suit
- ○ Scarf (*do rag*)
- ○ Belt
- ○ Clothes Pins
- ○ Sewing Kit
- ○ Hat

- ○ Other _____

- ○ Other _____

✓ Tools
- ○ Combination tool
- ○ Patch Kit
- ○ Screwdriver(s)
  - ○ Philips
    - ○ # 0
    - ○ # 1
    - ○ # 2
  - ○ Flat
    - ○ 5mm/ ^{3}/8 in
    - ○ 8mm/ ^{5}/8 in
- ○ Wrenches
  Hex, Open, Box
  or Sockets
  - ○ 4mm-H O B S
  - ○ 5mm-H O B S
  - ○ 6mm-H O B S
  - ○ 8mm-H O B S
  - ○ 9mm-H O B S
  - ○ 10mm-H O B S
- ○ 11mm-H O B S
  - ○ 12mm-H O B S
  - ○ 13mm-H O B S
  - ○ 14mm-H O B S
  - ○ Other_____
- ○ Pliers
- ○ Vise Grips
  - ○ 3in
  - ○ 5in
- ○ Cone Wrenches
- ○ Screws
- ○ Freewheel Remover
- ○ Crank Remover
- ○ Electrical Tape

EQUIPMENT LISTS

✓ Bicycle
○ Rear Rack
○ Front Rack
○ Low Riders
○ Rear Panniers
○ Handlebar Bag
○ Front Light
○ Rear Flashing Red
○ Light Other Color
○ Wiring for Lights
○ Generator
○ Batteries
○ Extra Batteries
○ Cables
   ○ Brake
   ○ Gears
○ Other_____
○ Special Screws
○ Special Screws
○ Cyclometer
○ Bungie Cords #_____
○ Other _____

○ _____

○ _____

○ _____

○ _____

○ _____

○ _____

○ _____

✓ Personal
○ Watch
○ Towel
○ Sunglasses
○ Helmet
○ First Aid Kit
○ Soap
○ Tooth Brush
○ Tooth Paste
○ Cosmetics
○ 2nd pair of
   Eyeglasses
○ Shaving
   Equipment
○ Medical
   Prescriptions
○ Eyeglass
   Prescription
○ Contact Lens
   Solutions
○ Journal
○ Citizenship ID
○ Pen
○ Stamps
○ Sun Screen
○ Medicine
○ Calculator
○ Flashlight
○ 25¢ (for phone)
○ Credit Cards
○ Passport & Visas
○ Tickets
○ Maps
○ Camera & Film
○ Photographs (self)

EQUIPMENT LISTS

✓ Camping
- ○ Tent
  - ○ Tent stakes
  - ○ Tent Poles
  - ○ Ground cloth
- ○ Rope (3m/10ft)
- ○ Sleeping Bag
- ○ Mattress
- ○ Day pack
- ○ H_2O Purifier/Filter
- ○ Toilet Paper
- ○ Candle
- ○ Flashlight
- ○ Other
- ○ _____

- ○ _____

✓ Cooking
- ○ Cup
- ○ Pot (Cook Set)
- ○ Knife
- ○ Fork
- ○ Spoon
- ○ Can
- ○ Opener/Cork Screw
- ○ Stove
  - ○ Fuel Bottle
  - ○ Fuel
  - ○ Matches
  - ○ Pre-Starter
- ○ Stove Repair Kit
- ○ Swiss Army Knife
- ○ Wire (2m/2yds)
- ○ Other _____

✓ Food
- ○ Pasta
- ○ Cereal
- ○ Rice
- ○ Dried Milk
- ○ Fruit
- ○ Cookies
- ○ Snacks

- ○ Other _____

- ○ _____

- ○ _____

- ○ Peanut Butter
- ○ Oil or fat
- ○ Vegetables _____
- ○ Vegetables _____
- ○ Vegetables _____
- ○ Other _____
- ○ _____

- ○ _____

- ○ _____

LESS IS MORE
LESS IS MORE

LESS IS MORE
LESS IS MORE

ORDER FORM

Cyclotour Guide Books publishes and distributes bicycle tour guide books and maps.

You can order our books and maps by checking the books you would like and then mailing or faxing this form to us. If the price of the book you order or the shipping charge changes then we will bill you for the increase/decrease in price.

The books listed on this Order Form are a sampling of the bicycle tour guide books we have in stock. Please look at our web site, www.cyclotour.com, for a complete description of all the books and maps we publish and distribute. You can order from the web site by sending an email to us: cyclotour@cyclotour.com

Please check the circle for the books you want.

○ 'Round Lake Ontario: A Bicyclist's Tour Guide,   us$24.95
○ 'Round Lake Michigan: A Bicyclist's Tour Guide   us$24.95
○ 'Round Lake Huron: A Bicyclist's Tour Guide   us$24.95
○ 'Round Lake Superior: A Bicyclist's Tour Guide   us$24.95
○ 'Round Lake Erie: A Bicyclist's Tour Guide   us$24.95
○ Erie Canal Bicyclist's & Hiker Tour Guide   us$24.95
○ Finger Lakes Bicyclist's Tour Guide   us$24.95
○ Editions Du Breil Guides to the French Canals   us$24.95 ea.
○ Pedallers' Paradise New Zealand Bike Guides   us$24.95 ea.
○ Cyclotours In & Around Stratford, Ontario   us$24.95
○ Rubel BikeMaps of Massachusetts   us$6.95 ea.

Book Sub-total

+   Per order shipping   us$4.30
(or current Priority Mail & Delivery Confirmation rate)

   Total

Shipping to addresses out side of the United States and its possessions is by US Postal Service Global Priority Mail. Go to www.usps.com to determine the large Global Priority Mail Envelope flat rate.

Your Name: _____

Your Address: _____

Your City, State/Prov., Zip/PC _____

Your Telephone Number _____
Send this form to: Or Telecommute it to:
Cyclotour Guide Books   Tel.: 585 244-6157
PO Box 10585   Fax: 585 244-6157
Rochester NY 14610-0585   email: cyclotour@cyclotour.com

Cyclotour Expense Log

Date	Odometer	Destination	Brkfast	Lunch	Dinner	Groceries	Snacks	Lodging	Bicycle	Misc.	Daily Total	Running Total
Total												

Cyclotour Expense Log

Date	Odometer	Destination	Brkfast	Lunch	Dinner	Groceries	Snacks	Lodging	Bicycle	Misc.	Daily Total	Running Total
Total												

Cyclotour Expense Log

Date	Odometer	Destination	Brkfast	Lunch	Dinner	Groceries	Snacks	Lodging	Bicycle	Misc.	Daily Total	Running Total
Total												

Date	Odometer	Destination	Brkfast	Lunch	Dinner	Groceries	Snacks	Lodging	Bicycle	Misc.	Daily Total	Running Total
Total												

Cyclotour Expense Log

BIBLIOGRAPHY

Altoff, Gerard T. *Deep Water Sailors, Shallow Water Soldiers: Manning the United States Fleet on Lake Erie, 1813*. Put-in-Bay, OH. The Perry Group. 1993.

Altoff, Gerard T. *Oliver Hazard Perry and the Battle of Lake Erie*. Put-in-Bay, OH: Perry Group. 1999.

Atticks, Kevin M. *Discovering Lake Erie Wineries: A Travel Guide to Lake Erie's Wine Country*. Baltimore, MD: Resonant Publishers. 2000.

DeHarpporte, Dean. *Northeast and Great Lakes Wind Atlas*. New York: Van Nostrand Reinhold. 1983.

Environment Canada and United States Environmental Protection Agency, et al. *The Great Lakes: An Environmental Atlas and Resource Book*. Chicago, IL and Toronto, ON: USEPA and Environment Canada. 1987.

Hatcher, Harlan H. *Lake Erie*. Indianapolis, IN, New York: Bobbs-Merrill. 1945.

Marchetti, Donna. *Around the Shores of Lake Erie: A Guide to Small Towns, Rural Areas and Natural Attractions*. Saginaw, MI: Glovebox Guidebooks of America. 1998.

Platt, Carolyn V. and Gary Meszros. *Birds of the Lake Erie Region*. Kent, OH: Kent State University Press. 2001.

Richardsons' Publishing. *Richardsons' Chartbook & Cruising Guide: Lake Erie including Lake St. Clair and Niagara River, 5th ed*. Chicago, IL: Richardsons' Publishing. 2000.

Roberts, Bruce and Ray Jones. *Eastern Great Lakes Lighthouses: Ontario, Erie, and Huron*. Guilford, CT: Globe Pequot Press. 2001.

Rosenberg, Max. *The Building of Perry's Fleet on Lake Erie, 1812-1813*. Harrisburg, PA: Pennsylvania Historical and Museum Commission. 1987.

Skaggs, David C. and Gerard T. Altoff. *A Signal Victory: The Lake Erie Campaign, 1812-1813*. Annapolis, MD:: Naval Institute Press. 2000.

Tanner, Helen Hornbeck, Adele Hast, Jacqueline Peterson, Robert J. Surtees, eds. and   Miklos Pinther, cartographer. *Atlas of Great Lakes Indian History, 1st ed*. Norman, OK: University of Oklahoma Press, Newberry Library. 1987.

Wachter, Georgann. *Erie Wrecks West: A Guide to Shipwrecks of Western Lake Erie, 2nd Ed*. Avon Lake, OH: CorporateImpact. 2001.

Wachter, Georgann. *Erie Wrecks East: A Guide to Shipwrecks of Eastern Lake Erie*. Avon Lake, OH.: CorporateImpact. 2000.

Wright, Matthew Michael, et al. *Lake Erie and Lake St. Clair Ports*

O'call. Evanston, IL: O'Meara-Brown Publications. 2002.

Bibliography from 1st Edition

Appleton, D., ed. *Appleton's Handbook of American Travel: Western Tour*. New York: D. Appleton. 1973.

Aylesworth, Thomas G. *Eastern Great Lakes*. New York: Chelsea House. 1988.

Cantor, George. *The Great Lakes Guide Book: Lakes Ontario and Erie*. Ann Arbor, MI: University of Michigan Press. 1985.

Derby, William. *A Tour From the City of New York to Detroit....* New York: Kirk & Merlem. 1918.

Diede, Alan. *Best Choices Along the Great Lakes Coast*. Pittsburgh, PA: Monongahelia Pub. Co. 1990.

Feldmann, Rodney R., Alan H. Coogan and Richard A. Heimlich. *Southern Great Lakes: Field Guide*. Dubuque, IA: Kendall/ Hunt. 1977.

Fitting, James, ed. *The Archeology of Michigan*. Garden City, NY: American Museum of Natural History (New York, NY). 1970.

Flint Institute of Art. *The Art of Great Lakes Indians*. Flint, MI: The Institute. 1973.

Geyer, Alan R. and William H. Bolles. *Outstanding Scenic Geological Features of Pennsylvania*. Harrisburg, PA: Commonwealth of Pennsylvania, Dep't. of Environmental Resources. 1979.

Hekin, Karl E. *Directory of Shipwrecks of the Great Lakes*. Boston, MA: Bruce Humphries Pub. 1966.

Jakle, John A. *Images of the Ohio Valley*. New York: Oxford University Press. 1977.

Johnson, Kathy. *Diving and Snorkeling Guide to the Great Lakes*. Houston, TX: Pices Books. 1990.

Lafferty, T., ed. *Ohio's Natural Heritage*. Columbus, OH: Ohio Academy of Sciences. 1976.

LesStrang, Jacques. *Cargo Carriers of the Great Lakes*. Boyne City, MI: Harbor House. 1985.

Nowicki, Tim. *Awake to Wildlife: The Complete Naturalist's Great Lakes Wildlife Almanac*. Clarkston, MI. 1994.

Stall, Cris. *Animal Tracks of the Great Lakes*. Seattle, WA: The Mountaineers. 1989.

Stewart, Darryl. *Point Pelee*. Don Mills, ON: Burns and MacEachem. 1977.

Urguhurt, Frederk A. *An Ecological Study of the Saltatoria of Point Pelee*. Toronto, ON: University of Toronto Press. 1981.

Van Diver, Bradford B. *Roadside Geology of New York*. Missoula, MT: Mountain Press. 1985.

INDEX